My Egypt:
Why I Left the Ex-Gay Movement

By Benjamin David

Also published by Yhabbut Publishing

Benjamin David

Pilgrim's Passage: A Rebuttal to Pilgrim's Progress
Left Out: What to Do if You're Left Behind or Left Below
My Egypt: Why I Left the Ex-Gay Movement

Ben Tousey

The Haunting of Holden Castle
The Warrior

Acknowledgments

I want to thank those who have supported me through the years.

My deepest thanks go to my mom, Sharon, who has encouraged me to write. She made huge sacrifices for me growing up when times were tough and raised us with an 'ear toward Heaven.'

I would also like to thank my sister, Anna. More than anyone else in the world, it was always Anna who reached out with a kind hand—not just to me, but to anyone around her who needed that kindness. Those who know her respect her for her compassion, wisdom, and diplomacy. For those she represented as a union president, she went to the wall for them, and most will never know how much she did to defend them. She's been more than a sister to me, she's been a friend. And now, as we walk this new path, we learn new ways to support each other.

I am also profoundly grateful for all she and her husband, Brendan, did for me in some of the darkest days of my life. In so many ways, she kept me alive and helped me stay afloat when I lost my footing. Every day I wish there was more I could do, something that would ease the pain. It's been a long, dark road for you, and I wish there was something I could do to soften the blows that keep coming.

And I'd also like to say, "I'm FUNNY, dammit!"

Brendan: Words can't describe how much I miss you. From the day my sister introduced us, I could see you were an amazing guy. In the decade I've known you, nothing has brought me greater joy than the way you took care of my little sister: honoring her, loving her, and bringing out the best in her.

> I also appreciate how much you did for our family and how you embraced the rest of us as if we were yours. You were generous, kind, and downright funny. Every picture I have of you shows you laughing, playing with children, playing with animals, making funny faces, and bringing happiness to

others (except for those pictures of you sleeping). Your reach was universal, and I consider myself extremely lucky to have known you... or... more likely, since your memory will always live with me... "to know you."

I miss you, buddy.
~ Cheers

Much of my writing was done in a place where I could still be around people but have my privacy too. There were people there who took such good care of me that I honestly don't how I could have written this without them: Amanda, Bobby, Kris, Randy, Maurice, Meghan, Slade, and Tye.

I would also like to send my very best to Drew. I've loved our chats, and I wish the best for you in your life.

Meghan and John, our Tini-nights are the highlight of my memories.

IN THE BEGINNING

It was late September 1984. Only a few days until I turned 19, and in Riverton, Wyoming, old enough to drink legally. I had spent most of my teenage life counting those days until I could walk into a bar, show my ID, and be ushered into the establishment, or purchase alcohol at a liquor store all by myself and not have to spend hours trying to find someone to buy it for me. My day of freedom was almost upon me, and I awaited it with fervent anticipation.

That was on my mind this evening as my younger sister, Rachel, her boyfriend, Pete, and I made our way in Pete's Gremlin from Riverton to Lander, a mere twenty-four miles away. Now Wyoming is nothing like most states as far as population. Riverton had a population of about 15,000, and Lander had a population of 8,000 (when Mrs. Barker's family was in town for the family reunion). Unlike today's modern cities, which go from town to town without leaving civilization, a trip between towns in Wyoming was lonely. Very few people and almost no artificial lights were on the roads this night.

Listening to AC/DC (my favorite band at the time) through Pete's stereo, deep inside me, something else was going on. Something so contrary to the outside world around me. Even though I was young (almost 19), I was exhausted and terrified that my friends would find out who I was. Deep inside, I was lonely and overcome with hopelessness.

As Pete drove his Gremlin (boy, did that have an excellent stereo system), I sat silently listening to the dulcet tones of "Hell's Bells" at a nearly deafening level—looking up through the clear autumn night: stars which were so bright and so thick, yet so far away. While looking at the sky at that moment, a thought crossed my mind, and I very quietly voiced it. "God," I said, "I don't know if I can change who I am, and I don't know if I want to. But if you want me *Just as I am*, I guess that's okay."

I looked at the stars, expecting them to fall toward the car or spell something grand in the sky, but nothing happened. A few stars winked, but it wasn't for me. Still, deep inside, as I stared up at the sky, with heavy metal blaring at ear-splitting volumes, something inside of me went still—a quiescence in a place that I hadn't felt for some time. I felt that maybe he did want me, even if I didn't know how to change. Pete noticed I had gotten quiet and said something about it, so I quickly rectified the situation by joining in with a rousing chorus of "You Shook Me All Night Long."

I never told anyone about that night, and we finished our trip to Lander and back just as we had started. By the time we returned to Riverton, that sense of peace was gone, but in its place, a small kernel of hope slowly took root in fertile, emotional soil.

Why Wouldn't God Want Me?

This is an interesting question. God is love, according to those who quote the Bible. *God so loved the world that he gave his only Son, that whoever believes in him shall not perish but have eternal life. John 3:16.* Yet implicitly, that promise didn't necessarily apply to everybody—specifically not to me (according to those around me).

I wasn't a murderer! I wasn't a thief (aside from the occasional candy bar). I wasn't a Satanist and didn't torture animals or make fun of children.

In the late 70s and early 80s, a guy named Mike Warnke entered the pantheon of Christian evangelists. Warnke was a "Christian comedian," and throughout his early career, he could attract crowds in the tens of thousands. A large part of his success was due to the fact that he claimed to be a Satanist who found Jesus.

Christians loved his testimony and ate it up like a tiger with raw meat.

Mike Warnke was welcome to the Kingdom of Heaven. But not me.

I did have problems. I drank—a lot. I had issues with drugs—lots of issues. I'd been kicked out of several Evangelical Christian schools. My mom and stepdad fought most of the time (over me). I was a partier (and a bit of a mooch); to the adults around me, I was the "bad seed." I lied to my parents about where I was going at night, and I sometimes stole money to buy alcohol. I wasn't easy to live with, and I knew that. And I loved disco. But most kids around me had even bigger problems, and God loved them.

What I *did* was nothing compared to what Mike Warnke—the Satanist—claimed to have done. So what could be worse than being a Satanist?

It wasn't *what*, but *who*, and I was that man.

In the Beginning... God

My story begins and ends with God: the reason for my problem and the solution simultaneously.

As I looked up at the stars that night, I contemplated a sin with such a stigma that I couldn't talk about it to anyone. Not even God hissself. I was an eighteen-year-old man who wanted to have sex. *What eighteen-year-old didn't?* But I was different. I wanted to have sex with a man—someone of my own gender.

In high school, while my guy friends were dating girls, I wanted to date my guy friends. I had a girlfriend or two to throw everyone off the scent, but eventually, it became too frustrating for both of us, and there were some hard feelings. While my guy friends bragged about their sexual exploits, I had to make mine up and never let it slip that I was jealous of their girlfriends.

I knew God heard my prayer that night in Pete's Gremlin because of a minor 'miracle' a few days later. All my life, I wanted to write songs. I was a pianist, but even more than that, I wanted to be a songwriter. Until then, most of my writing was hardly noteworthy *(no pun intended),* and I knew my songs were armature. On this night, days after my prayer, a melody came to me as I was sitting at the piano playing random chords and notes. It blossomed in my head, through my fingers, and onto the keyboard. As the melody flowed, so did the song lyrics. I ran quickly, got some paper and a pen, and started writing as fast as possible to keep up.

Within an hour, I had a song. This particular song was what I would call my *'first real song'*; the first melody I ever wrote with any substance. It was far advanced from all my other musical musings. Many other, better songs would follow, but this was my first.

The lyrics also told me God had heard my prayer because it was called "Coming Home Again," and it reflected my feelings of abandoning childhood beliefs in God and striking out to find a 'happier' life that somehow kept eluding me. It was a story about the Prodigal Son, abandoning his father, only to return when he could no longer handle things in the cold world.

But the second verse was God talking to me, telling me that as lonely as I felt running, he felt lonely waiting. The chorus for the first verse was, *"This loneliness is killing me."* The chorus for the second verse was, *"Loneliness it killed me too."*

As I played and sang, my eyes welled up with tears. I was home again. God and I were reconciled. He did want me, and he was showing me this by giving me my first song.

I was about to embark on a journey deep into the heart of God, further than I ever wanted to go—and so deep I would never be able to climb out again.

IT WAS YOUR FATHER'S FAULT

This statement is a double entendre since there are two fathers at play in this narrative. One was my natural father, and the other was God—and my relationship with both was troubled to say the least. It becomes more complicated when you add my mom's subsequent boyfriends and her marriage to my stepdad. Let's be clear. My mom's taste in men has always been dreadful for her and her kids.

So when the Exodus organization suggests that homosexuality is caused by the breakdown of father/son—male/male relationships, in my case, it made sense.

You've probably heard my story if you've spent much time in Christian circles. You've heard all the testimonies. So many times that when you think about hearing it again, your eyes glaze over, and you start dreaming of Amy Grant in a tight-fitting halo.

This common misconception among the antigay community that homosexuality is caused by the breakdown of the father/son or mother/daughter relationships is an idea popularized by Elizabeth Moberly in her book, *Homosexuality: A New Christian Ethic*. She labeled it *"defensive detachment."* Her thesis assumed that if there was a breakdown in these relationships, the child would seek to "repair" these wounds by trying to have sex with members of their own gender. Her cure, therefore, was to form close but non-sexual, same-sex friendships. However, she only thought this should happen in groups because it never crossed her mind that two gay men or two gay women could hang out together without somehow hooking up. She assumed that the only contact gay people had with each other was sexual.

This is not only a lie, but it's also impossible. Just because we're gay doesn't mean we all get along. It just means we share commonalities regarding sexuality. Like straight people, many of us don't even share the same taste in men or women.

I don't remember much about my childhood and even less about my relationship with my natural father. I spent large portions of my earlier life either not thinking about it or trying to stay detached from it. New 'revelations' did show up occasionally, though, especially as I tried to rid myself of the dread curse of sexuality.

One thing I do know, however, is that I've met a lot of people over my lifetime, and with only a few exceptions, most of them had bad relationships with their fathers/mothers—and they aren't gay.

My memories of God, on the other hand, are much clearer. Most of my memories start after my mom and dad divorced *(I was six)*, but I remember being into Jesus. He was a big brother. He liked me, and I loved him, and I loved talking about him. Needless to say, it annoyed the hell out of the adults around me who were always telling me to shut up—more accurately, STFU.

As with any life story, I started out young and innocent. I was born in a hospital in Whitefish, Montana, and everything went downhill. I was the oldest of three kids: myself, Rachel (the only girl and the middle child), and Brian, the youngest. We were born relatively close together, with only fourteen months separating me and my sister and barely three years separating me and my younger brother, Brian.

Before he was even one, it was discovered that Brian had been born with a heart defect. They caught it early, but there was no question that he would have to eventually have surgery to try to repair it—sooner rather than later.

My sperm donor... a.k.a. my father, was a vagrant. My earliest memories are of living in a small white-trash trailer with a lean-to built onto it. Our bathroom was an outhouse, and we had to haul water from a creek behind the trailer for drinking, laundry (which my mom did by hand), and cooking. Our nearest neighbor was a mile-and-a-half away.

We lived in Olney, Montana, on the backside of Glacier National Park. We were often told not to go outside because bears had wandered into the yard looking for food. Some days I would go outside to see deer and, in the evening, raccoons. Skunks were everywhere at night, and I saw my first garter snake there. I watched my mom beat the life out of the poor thing with the bottom of a shovel. Rats, too, were in plenteous supply.

My father was a pilot and owned a small airplane. When he wasn't flying planes, he was jumping out of them. He was a skydiver. And after their jumps, he and his friends would all go to their favorite bar in Kalispell to binge-drink it up. He spent much of his time at the local airport with his skydiving buddies, at the bar, or his girlfriend's house.

In many ways, this was a blessing. He was a drinker, quick to anger, violent, and verbally, physically, and emotionally abusive. And he didn't like me. He never came out and said those exact words, but he accused me of being a momma's boy (the same mom he beat mercilessly when angry), called me worthless, and laughed when the other kids beat me up. What I remember the most about that time was confusion. Why did he have so much animosity toward me? Of course, that's how I frame it now. Back then, it was, "I'm a horrible boy to make Daddy so angry!" And then I'd punish myself.

He even told my mom many times that he didn't like me because I was too much like her—the woman he married. He hated her. He chose to have a child yet hated that child once it was born.

I was a mellow toddler, according to my mom. I liked sitting in my little rocking chair and listening to music for hours. Mostly classical. I also got along with animals. My parents had friends who owned a Siberian Husky, and I would play with her for hours, just petting, walking, and adoring her. (To this day, the Husky is my favorite breed). When she had puppies, she was, like most moms, very protective and wouldn't allow anyone near them for the first few weeks. Yet, one night, I disappeared. When my parents and their friends found me, I was sitting in her box, playing with her puppies. She was growling low, but she never hurt me. She trusted me.

Note: I wish I understood what that meant, to have that trust from an animal. That isn't given easily, and it was contrary to so much of what I had been told about myself growing up.

One of my strongest memories of my father happened when I was just five or six. I was in my room listening to him, and my mother fight in the kitchen. I remember him yelling, and then I heard the sound of a slap. After which, I heard dishes fall and knew he must have knocked her over. I remember being seized with terror. She was hurt, but I could do nothing to help her. It remains one of the most helpless feelings I've ever had.

When I was six, my mom discovered my dad's affair and filed for divorce. After this, the Sperm Donor moved in with his girlfriend. I rarely saw him after that. It's not that I didn't want to see him. I did. But he didn't want to see me. I didn't understand the dynamics since I was too young, but I remember how I felt to some degree. Aside from an occasional visit to the airport, where he hung out, and an occasional camping trip, that was all I saw of him. Which, as I said, is where my earliest memories of God start to show up.

God would try to become what my father would not be: attentive, present, and available. If I lost something, I told God about it. If I was afraid, I told God about it. I remember often leaving my bike unattended and "plead the blood of Jesus around it." Nothing ever happened to it, so I assumed my relationship with God and Jesus was solid. Jesus was my older brother, God was my father, and both looked out for me like fathers and big brothers do.

I mention older brother because I really wanted one of those throughout my life. I wanted a male older than me, wiser than me, to look after, protect, and take care of me. One of my strongest memories is when I was entering high school. I checked out a young-adult book from the library. I do not remember the book's name, but I remember the cover. On the cover, a boy who looked about fourteen was looking out at me, and behind him was his brother, probably about seventeen, standing over his brother with his arms over the shoulders and hands clasped in front of his chest.

That image has stuck with me to this day.

I think I took to God because those around me were miserable and hurtful, and I was desperate for love. In particular, a *loving* father. I often started my prayers with, "Dear Daddy..." I had a massive daddy-sized hole in my heart, and God would be the plaster of Paris that would *"try"* to fill that void.

After the divorce, my mom worked a series of jobs. We moved a lot, including into a trailer in Kalispell, where she worked at a convenience store just up the road. By the time I was seven, I had moved five times. I moved from our shanty in Olney, MT, to the White House in Whitefish, to the Gray House in Evergreen, to her Pontiac car, and then to the trailer in Kalispell.

Since my mom didn't make enough money to keep up with the bills, she went on welfare so we could at least get food and pay rent. My father had been required to pay child support, but he refused and told my mother that he would rot in jail before paying a dime. Since it was Montana in the 1970s, nobody was going to enforce child support, so we went hungry. One day when I was about seven or eight, I went without food for so long that I started throwing up and passed out on the bathroom floor. Someone fed me a piece of government cheese, which boosted my blood sugar levels, and I was okay after that.

After the divorce, my mom hit the bars, and several men were in and out of her trailer. Some were one-night stands, and some we got to know for a while. A lot of them were abusive.

It never occurred to me that this might not be how other kids lived.

My sister, Rachel, remembers several shouting matches between my mom and my grandfather over how we kids were being raised (I have no recollection of them). And it was for that reason that my grandfather stepped in to try and help. He would come and get us on weekends and take us to stay with him and my grandmother. They lived in Summers, MT, and had a house on Flathead Lake. They took us out for pizza and had good food in their cupboards. They had a massive yard for us to play in and a satellite to watch good T.V. (primarily cartoons). My grandfather bought a riding lawnmower and let me mow the lawn... it was such a difference between what we experienced at home.

My grandfather became a surrogate father. We didn't talk about much, but we did things. I went with him to take garbage to the dump. I played in the frigid lake while he worked on his boat. He took me fishing (which I hated. I couldn't sit still that long.), and I'd hang out in the garage while he futzed around with his tools fixing things that probably never needed to be fixed. And in the evening, we'd watch M*A*S*H together. To this day, it's my favorite television show.

As a kid, it never entered my mind what was happening. I just liked spending time with my grandparents.

Gramps was a bit gruff and often impatient. He'd already raised four kids and was now stuck with three more. I don't remember ever talking about anything with him. I didn't like sports, he hated my taste in music (which I was never allowed to play at his house), and let's face it... I could be a petulant child.

As a kid, this worked for us. But things would change radically as I became a tweenager and then a teenager. For one thing, so many people in my life were brutally chipping away at my self-esteem. My dad, of course. He made fun of me when I couldn't defend myself and beat the snot out of me when I tried.

My mom also went off on tirades, beating us for various infractions. To this day, one of my strongest childhood memories is me sitting in my bedroom in our trailer in Kalispell, and I wrote in bold letters, "I HATE MOM!" I do not remember what she did or what happened, but I vividly remember the anger. I was raging in that way where it felt like it would force itself out of my body.

Teachers didn't help my self-esteem at this point, either. In the second grade, I had a teacher who took great pleasure in deriding me and making fun of my inability to understand assignments. I do not remember the teacher's name, only that she was meaner than a hornet after its hive had been disturbed. She loved embarrassing me in front of the class for not knowing the answers to questions.

However, she was nothing compared to my third-grade teacher, Mrs. Jackson—one of the vilest human beings on the planet. She was to children what the wicked witch was to Hansel and Gretel—only Montana law forbade her from roasting children in a fire. Instead, she had to work out her vitriol in other ways.

For some reason, I was always in trouble with her. One time she paddled me in front of the class because I was playing tag with a girl on the playground. It was your typical horseplay. The girl would tag me, and then I would chase her, and vice versa. Another time she made me stand with my nose in the corner because I was reading upside down. That was something I discovered I could do relatively easily, and so I did it. When she realized what I was doing, she embarrassed me and put me in the corner. Another time she made me sing to the whole class because I didn't have anything for show and tell. I will never forget her as the worst teacher/human being I've ever encountered (and I've met some pretty awful people).

During this school year, my mom was also involved in a serious car accident. She fell asleep at the wheel (she had Narcolepsy, but it was late at night, so other questions came up, too) and rolled her car down a steep embankment. She was injured, but fortunately, it wasn't fatal. Unfortunately, I remember visiting her in the hospital and receiving a cold reception—though I didn't understand why.

When I was eight, my mom "got born-again..." which meant I got born-again too. She started hanging around a group who were part of the *Jesus People* movement, which meant that her children were hanging around them too. A handful of men and women lived together in a large house on a farm outside of Kalispell. I don't know if the farm was owned by one of the group members or if they rented it, but it was a popular place for people to hang out.

I liked my mom's friends for the most part, but a couple of memories troubled me when they happened and have never left me since. The most striking happened with my brother, Brian. My mom was driving, Bruce was in the passenger seat, and the three kids were in the back seat. But ironically, I remember it as if I were in the driver's seat. My mom had parked the car and gone to run an errand. Brian was acting up, as Brian often did, and Bruce pulled him over the seat and paddled Brian's ass with his hand.

Maybe it was the suddenness of the act, or maybe it was the perceived violence of the act, or maybe it was the attack on someone I loved deeply, but I was stunned. How dare someone who isn't my mother attack my brother, especially since he was struggling with a heart defect.

When I turned ten, my mother met and married Roger, a friend of a friend. Roger was Seventh-day Adventist which meant I was now Adventist as well. All of a sudden, I found myself banned from Saturday morning cartoons, pepperoni pizza, and Coke *(SDAs pretend to observe the Jewish sabbath, eschew pork, and aren't allowed to drink caffeine. I like to call them 'Jewish wannabes afraid to commit).* But at the ripe old age of ten-ish, I discovered I had joined the *"true church"* that would usher Jesus into the New Age.

I went from belonging to a family that consisted of a mom and three kids to a mom, stepdad, three kids, and two stepsisters. I didn't like Roger, nor did I like my two stepsisters. Roger was a journeyman, kind of a Jack-of-all-trades. He was technically a carpenter. He framed houses, poured concrete, plastered walls and ceilings, laid insulation, remodeled, and even worked with the electrical and plumbing.

Looking back, I don't think I had a problem with his work (though I was never a fan of that kind of work). I think it was just that I didn't like Roger. I wanted to be an actor and a musician and saw 'drama' in almost everything around me. It was all about the story (or a story). I LOVED stories so much that I often put myself in the middle of any tale I was either reading or hearing. My favorite story at that time (to a large degree now) was C.S. Lewis's The Horse and His Boy from "The Chronicles of Narnia."

Of course, these were a stupid waste of time to Roger, and he had no problem making that known to me, my mom, and those around me—especially in the church.

I vividly remember the first time I met his eldest daughter (my younger stepsister). My cousin (about my age) and I were playing in a pile of dirt in my cousin's backyard. We were building roads, driving sticks on them as if they were cars, and then collapsing dirt on them and pretending they were buried under a landslide—typical boy stuff for that age.

A girl approached us. She knew my cousin, but I didn't know who this girl was. I'd never met her. I think she was mad that my cousin wouldn't play with her. She approached me and my cousin and started making a scene. She started yelling, kicking dirt at us, stomping on our roads, and throwing our sticks away.

Both my cousin and I got so angry that we stood up to deal with her face-to-face. At which point she ran to her father and hid behind him where we couldn't get to her.

I was furious. I hated her instantly and hoped I would never see her again. But it was only a few days later that her father and his two girls were at our house, and he and my mom were getting friendly.

After a few weeks of dating, Roger moved us into a one-bedroom shack behind his woodshop. *(For those counting, this is now six times.)* The shop was halfway between Columbia Falls, and Whitefish, Montana, about thirty miles from Kalispell. This would be our home for at least a couple of years. This shop was filled with Roger's tools, and it was filthy. There was sawdust everywhere, tools strewn about, and every counter space was in complete and utter disarray... and it was my job to clean it. The problem was that it was only a few hours before it was a total mess again.

Reminiscent of my father's house, there was no running water in this shack, and the only heat we had was a wood stove in the basement, which we could barely get to because the basement, like his shop, was filthy and cluttered with damp sawdust that reached almost to the surface of the furnace. We used the wood scraps from Roger's shop to burn, which was how we heated the place. The back of the shack, and the living quarters, would get warm-ish, but the shop never would, and I was expected to be in that shop for hours every day helping Roger with his work, cleaning, and doing other chores. This wasn't a big deal in the summer, but in the winter, Montana could get extremely cold.

In the back was one bedroom where all seven of us slept. There was a bed for my mom and Roger and two bunk beds. Two of my sisters had to share a bed. Aside from the bedroom, there was a kitchen and a bathroom with a curtain for a door. So every day, we would make the trip from the bedroom, down the hall to the kitchen to eat, and then go back to the room to sit or into the shop to work. On the upside, we weren't being polluted by all that trash on TV since we didn't have one.

Again, not knowing better, I thought this was normal.

On Saturdays (the Sabbath), we were carted off to Sabbath school and then on to the church in Kalispell since, as a specialty church, there was only one in what they call the Flathead Valley. Nearly every Saturday in Sabbath School, our teacher would drum into our heads that God had called Ellen G. White to be his "last days" prophet and that the church she built was the only true church that would survive the great persecution. Were I, or any of us, to turn our backs on the true church, we would burn in the Lake of Fire at the end of days. This also meant leaving the Adventist church to join another church.

Note: Adventists didn't believe in an everlasting hell. They believed there would be a prolonged persecution of the Adventists by the Antichrist (the Pope and the Catholic Church), and then Jesus would return and take them to Heaven. When Jesus returned, all the evil would die, and Satan and his minions would roam the Earth for a thousand years with no one to tempt, which was supposed to be awful for him. He would also have a thousand years to view the destruction he caused humankind.

At the end of those thousand years, The New Jerusalem would descend from Heaven, the Mount of Olives would flatten, and the city would rest on top of the Old Jerusalem. All the dead would rise and see all the Adventists nestled snugly in the New Jerusalem. Satan would have one last chance to tempt humankind, and all humanity would then attack the New Jerusalem to try and overtake the city.

Once they were all in place, God would call fire from Heaven, which would consume them. They would be gone forever, never to be remembered ever again. It would be as if they never existed in the first place.

This was all disturbing imagery to a young boy. I used to envision standing outside New Jerusalem because I went to a movie, ate a pepperoni pizza, drank a Pepsi, or watched Bugs Bunny on a Saturday.

Suddenly my relationship with God became more complicated. The God I had known up to this point was pretty laid back and easygoing. He always loved me, and there was never anything between us. He didn't expect that much from me except to just be me. I did not need to hide anything from him and could talk to him about anything.

But thanks to Roger and the SDA Church, all that changed. This new God was austere. He could get mad at me for drinking caffeine and watching cartoons on Saturday; if I went to another church, he would disown me altogether. Forever gone was my gentle and kindhearted father. God went from unconditional love to very conditional love.

As I mentioned, my little brother was three years younger than me and was born with a severe heart defect. We all knew about this, but Brian managed to function normally for the first part of his life. However, as he reached six and seven, the heart defect started taking its toll on his little body, and he was sent to Children's Hospital at the University of Washington in Seattle for surgery. Brian died the night after the surgery, and when I was ten years old, I learned that my little brother would never come home again. I'll never forget that day or that phone call. I was staying with my aunt Mary in Montana, and my mom called from Seattle to tell me that "Brian was sleeping with Jesus." (*Adventists also believe that the dead stay dead until Jesus returns, and then they all rise together with the living to meet Jesus in the air at the second coming.*) Still, no matter how I thought of it, it hurt. Sleeping with Jesus or not, he was never waking up.

My grandfather took me to view Brian's body at the funeral home. I could touch it. His face was expressionless, his eyes were closed, and despite his body being right there in front of me, he was not. I found this disturbing.

My relationship with God had just taken another big hit.

We had prayed for Brian incessantly for years. We claimed the promise that God wanted, above all things, that we should prosper and be in health. We believed that Jesus healed, and we believed that he was going to heal Brian. Yet there he was, lifeless in front of me.

After Brian's death, I learned what kind of man my father really was. He paid for Brian's funeral and then deducted the funeral costs from the child support he owed my mother (which he had never paid). Roger wasn't much better. He couldn't wait to spend all the money pouring in from friends and family members to convey their sympathies and help offset funeral costs.

Shortly after Brian's death, when I was 10, Roger took a job with the Seventh-day Adventist Church as a Bible Salesman selling Ellen G. White Books in Lander, Wyoming. So the family was moved to our new residence in Lander, Wyoming, from Kalispell, Montana, where the extended family lived—our family of four children (now down by one), my mom, and Roger. Our family added bulk to the little Adventist church and church school directly behind the church. I was now up to 8 moves in 11 years.

There's no question in my mind that there was a breakdown in the father/son relationship—at least in my life. The man who was my father and the man who stepped into my father's role were both far from skilled in their parenting abilities. Emotionally, I longed for a "real" — "loving" father. Still, I wasn't fatherless. My grandfather was there after my mom divorced my dad and until we moved to Wyoming. After the move, though, I would see a lot less of him because of the distance.

I suspect that the assumption about the breakdown of the father/son relationship that "causes" the men to "turn" gay probably works quite a bit differently than ex-gay groups think it does. It appears as if a straight father, especially a macho shithead like my father or Roger, may recognize that their son isn't "macho" like them. So they, in turn, start pulling away from the child (like my father, who thought I was too much like my mom, or Roger, who rejected me because I wasn't a man). Maybe the differences were already visible—at least on a subconscious level, and that's what created the distance.

It's kind of a "which came first..." scenario.

My Milkshake Comes to the Yard

Before my mom met Roger, but after she became born again, she met two ladies in a Pentecostal church we attended. Bernadette and Brenda were trying to start a music ministry. We loved B and B. I don't recall ever seeing them apart.

As a kid, once again, they looked 'normal.' But looking back, they remind me of a Lilith Fair concert. They were big ladies who played their guitars and sang together—folk music. They traveled and lived in a large motor home, whether to church for gigs, to our trailer to sing to us privately, or to go to the shopping store (do you see a pattern here?).

I can't say positively that they were lovers. It was Kalispell, Montana, and they wanted to start a music ministry in the church. However, as I look back, I can't help but wonder.

"Why do I wonder?" you might ask.

"Because," I will answer. "I can't help but wonder if the Universe was attempting to prepare me in any way for the journey that I was going to be taking," and if it was, did I "get it"? And the answer is "No! I didn't get it." At least not right away.

When Roger moved us to Lander, Wyoming, we kids were placed into a Seventh-day Adventist church school. I'll never forget Mrs. Gordon, our teacher. She was probably in her early thirties, with graying peppered hair. The one-room school was small and attached to the church, consisting only of a handful of families. Of course, the two most prominent families were ours, four kids (now minus Brian) and the Garrets (who had six kids, although only two attended school with me.

Though it was small, this school was overrun with politics gone awry. The parents of the students were more childish than the students (we had to get it from somewhere). While I never heard her say anything, looking back, it must have made Mrs. Gordon's life hell. She only lasted two years before finding a new gig, and I can't say I blame her. But she was amazing to me. Maybe that was because she saw something in me that I was not yet aware of but was beginning to express itself in ways I was too naïve to know.

Mrs. Gordon came to Wyoming from Iowa. In Iowa, she had a roommate who, she told us all, would be joining her in Lander soon. When Marsha arrived—there's just no gentle way to say this—she was butch. Looking back, Marsha was the stereotypical lesbian. She lived in blue jeans at least three sizes too small and mainly wore flannel shirts. She kept her hair super short and combed over and talked and gestured like the women who hung out with Dykes on Bikes.

And we loved her, too. Roger used to think he was quite the mechanic, but Marsha was, hands-down, the best mechanic in town. And there wasn't a bicycle in our school that she couldn't fix (and she loved doing it for us). And often is the time she would bend over to look at a bicycle chain or a spoke, and there was a half-moon shining proudly for all to see. There were other things that I could see looking back, like how they behaved around each other. The way they wrestled in the snow that one day they came to our house to announce that school was being canceled because of the snow. The way they sometimes stole glances at each other when we kids were at recess.

It is entirely possible that I threw this milkshake on them by misremembering, and I have spent a great deal of time going through those memories to make sure it was my yard, and their life, was better than yours...

By the time I hit sixth grade, certain changes had started to take place. I can only name these changes in retrospect because I wasn't even aware of many of them at the time. Nor did I know the changes were hitting me differently than my fellow students.

I remember talking to my mom one day, and she asked me why I "threw my wrist" when I talked. I didn't realize I was doing that, so I immediately started paying attention to how I used my hands to gesture. One day, out of the blue, she and Roger asked me if I knew how gay men had sex. I didn't even know how straight men had sex. I didn't know the difference between gay and straight. Those words meant something entirely different to me, so I had no idea how to answer them. But I knew something was wrong, and there must be a reason they were asking me this. So, again, I panicked.

But why? What was so frightening?

The adults around me were also starting to behave toward me in a colder and more hostile way. I remember one night in a car with Roger and our pastor, parked in front of a liquor store. I remember thinking out loud about what it would be like if an earthquake suddenly hit and all the bottles of alcohol crashed onto the floor. This had nothing to do with how I felt about alcohol because I didn't care about it one way or the other. The Adventist church had real problems with it, but I didn't give it much thought. Most of my family were heavy drinkers, so that was all just typical for me. What I was wondering, though, is what it would look like to watch all those bottles shake and then swing and finally fall on the floor and shatter, spilling booze everywhere.

After saying this, the pastor said out loud, "I guess there's hope for Benny after all."

Another surprise. It never occurred to me that I had fallen so far. Did they feel this way because I was weird (which I would say mainly was true) or if I was evil? And HOW was I evil?

Mrs. Gordon must have recognized something in me. While I've never been able to confirm it, anecdotally, I think it is true. It was the way she treated me. Rather than make digs about my odd behavior as other church members would, she seemed to encourage me in her own little ways. One day, I had a meltdown and got in trouble with the teacher's aide. When Mrs. Gordon returned, she wasn't happy with me. As she was chastising me, something happened, and despite every effort to control myself, I broke down and started to cry. She was there immediately with her arms around me, trying to comfort me. When she would catch me in "good behavior," she would reward me (and the class) with buttons we could redeem for cheesy toys she bought with her own money. When nobody else was around, she would give me simple advice about how important it was for me to be myself. And I remember her encouraging me to bathe more often in a very kind and silly way.

Meanwhile, my relationship with Roger was steadily going downhill. However, there was nobody I could talk to about it since Roger was a respected elder in the church, and we weren't allowed to talk about our problems.

Well, that's not entirely true. Roger had carte blanche to talk about us all he wanted, and he did. And I was his biggest problem.

Roger was violent and abusive the day I met him, but at first, he didn't 'hit' outside of spankings. He did scream and berate, though, and he could say some pretty ugly things. Yet the more time we spent together, the more that changed.

One of our biggest contentions was music. Growing up, my mom listened to the classics, The Rolling Stones, Led Zeppelin, The Dave Clark 5. She had a lot of rock and roll albums, and I loved rock and roll, so I would listen to it every chance I got. This angered Roger because "I was deliberately putting the family into the middle of God's wrath and risking inviting Satan into our home.

Naturally, this made no sense to me. I was covered in the blood of Jesus and therefore protected from God's wrath. God would never allow Satan to step into a Christian's home. Yet this is not what Adventists believe (or Evangelicals, for that matter), and they chipped away at my sense of protection so that I would take God's fury seriously.

Rock and roll was an incarnation of Satan worship, and disco (which came out a little later) caused and fostered homosexuality in laboratory rats. (No joke. They had studies.) Christian rock was worse. It was Satan infiltrating the church. They told the story often about the missionaries in Africa who were playing their Christian rock in Africa, and one day the villagers told them that their music contained the same beat that the villagers used to call the devil in their rituals. One lady in our church, in particular, quoted Ellen G. White as saying that "the beat of Africa" would infiltrate God's church. However, I've never found this quote, but she used it a lot.

Music was, and always will be, how I deal with life that seems so out of control.

Amid all this drama, our family dysfunction continued to worsen, and Roger was learning how to play on the sympathy of the church.

I was never one for subtlety. If I was angry, it was hard to hide it. If I was having a problem, I didn't smile through the trials. I suffered out loud. I was sent home from school many times during my junior high years. Despite how much Mrs. Gordon liked me, my behavior was still too much for her to take sometimes.

In my last year of Junior High, Mrs. Gordon left Lander (can you blame her?), and in came Mr. Davies. This guy was bizarre. There's just no other way to describe him.

Still, the Universe has a bizarre sense of humor. During that period, Roger learned that his ex-wife and the mother of his daughters was living with her lesbian lover. Of course, we never told anyone about it for fear of the ensuing scandal, but it was a topic of constant conversation in our house. Roger couldn't believe it. He continued to say that. "I just can't believe it." She had left the church and was determined to take the express route to Hell, and Roger was disgusted by it... or was he?

So it looked like the milkshake was all around me, although I didn't know it.

Meanwhile, God was still my buoy. He was my go-to. I could talk to him anytime about anything. And I did.

Ellen G. White was considered God's last-days prophet in the Adventist church, so I read her books. Because I was too young to know better, I took her word as gospel. I would also fantasize about being a prophet myself. Something deep inside me wanted to be recognized as spiritually wise. I wanted that relationship with God that Ellen White claimed to have. I wanted that relationship with God that the prophets had. I wanted to hear God's voice. I wanted to see God's face. I remember reading one day in my Bible that if you were to look upon God's face, you would die, and I remember thinking, "What a way to go." I wanted to look upon God's face and die. It would all be worth it to me.

I loved Bible stories. In my mind, they came to life (remember the Roman soldier?). I put myself into them in such a way that it never made sense to me that Eve could have possibly trusted a snake. "What was she thinking?" Now if it were a Kuala bear, that would make more sense, but everyone knew that snakes were creepy crawly things, and they lay in wait and then would bite. I was enamored with the story of David and Jonathan. There was something about their relationship that I was drawn to. Being naïve still, I didn't realize what was going on emotionally, but it was pulling at those emotional needs. I used to fantasize about having a friend like Jonathan, who was so close that we could physically hold each other. It hadn't led to anything sexual since I didn't even know what sex was, but the emotional black hole was massive, pulling at anything that might get too close.

Despite all this, or because of all this, I was considered rebellious by Roger and his church friends. I couldn't imagine a God who didn't like rock and roll. That was inconceivable to me. At that time, Grease, with John Travolta and Olivia Newton-John, was big, and I couldn't stop singing "You're the One that I Want." I had chills, and they were multiplying.

Note: We moved three times in Lander. First TO Lander and into Garrett's house. Then to the house on Main Street, and finally to the duplex across the street from the Adventist School, bringing the total of moves up to eleven moves in 13 years.

IT'S NOT A CHOICE... IT'S A DISCOVERY

It's the hymn of the Christian whenever the topic of homosexuality arises, and it's usually sung by people who have had minimal contact with homosexuals (or at least never listened to them). "Homosexuality is a choice," they intone in their best James Dobson voice. But up until now, I hadn't made any choices along those lines. It's not like I opened my underwear drawer and asked, "What shall I wear today, and what sexuality shall I be?

What person in their right mind would choose to go through what most gay men and women go through in their lives? We've all tried dating the opposite sex, only to wind up hurting those we love. That's not how we want to be in this world. We have to watch every word we say lest we give ourselves away. And we never know which pronouns to use when talking about our friends. We're abused, denied pizza, wedding cake, Websites, and simple human dignity.

We didn't choose this.

The first indication in my memory of being "different" from my friends was after seeing the movie Grease in high school. During the movie, I could not stop looking at John Travolta. He was so good-looking, so athletic, and so masculine. At first, I thought it was just envy. I thought I just wanted to be like him. but I was also observing how he looked in his tight pants and leather jacket. After the movie, when all the boys were talking about Olivia Newton-John in her tight leather and going on about how sexy she was, I suddenly realized that something was very wrong. I wasn't affected by her at all. Okay, her look was flawless, and she could sing, but that's where it ended for me. So I joked with my friends about how hot she was and tried to ignore the other feelings the movie had stirred up.

It wasn't long after that when I had my first wet dream. Guess who played the starring role in the erotic Dreamplay? You guessed it—John Travolta.

As time went on, it became apparent to me that things weren't going to change. I was now keenly aware of the testosterone around me. I found myself looking at guys when I thought they wouldn't notice.

I was shipped off to Campion Academy in Loveland, Colorado, during my freshman year in high school. (Do I count this as a move? This would put me at 12.) Campion was a four-year boarding school for Adventists so that we could avoid being indoctrinated by the false teaching outside the church—and we would be safe from any heretical teaching that even used the same letters as those found in the word "evolution."

My first few weeks at Campion were pretty uneventful, but something happened that changed all of that. When I first arrived at Campion, I didn't know anyone, was far away from home, and was extremely shy (okay, not extremely, but I hated not knowing anyone and was afraid to reach out). I was also going through that awkward time in my life where hormones were churning, the body was changing, and I was forced to deal with the ups and downs of being a teenager without anyone telling me what was happening. I felt profoundly out of place. I had no idea that much of this was natural. I thought I was experiencing something that nobody else was, and that experience was wrong.

I lived in a dormitory surrounded by other guys. I had a guy as a roommate. I showered with guys. I went to the bathroom with guys. I had my devotions with guys. There were guys all around me, and the school set it up so that guys and girls didn't have too many opportunities to get too close. It was also in this setting that I became aware of sexual feelings. Until then, I had been relatively naïve about the subject, even with my unexplainable feelings toward John Travolta, but at Campion, things were getting more complicated. I was now a teenager, and I was sexually agitated. Still, I was careful never to let my guard down for fear of the consequences.

Somehow, no matter how hard we try not to, we must emit some fairy dust, or everyone around us has some Fairy Sensory Perception (FSP) because the people around us seem to know, regardless of our best efforts to hide it. I was standing outside the boy's dormitory one day, between the dorm and the cafeteria, and Tony and his friends were there. I was waiting for my friend to join me to go to the cafeteria for supper. Four of us stood there: me, Tony, and the two friends he traveled with. I looked over at Tony, and when I did, he shot back an icy stare, and with all the venom he could muster, he spit out the word, "Faggot!" That was the defining moment... that was it. I now knew what I was. I was a faggot.

I stood on the sidewalk looking over at Tony, completely stunned. I didn't know what to say.

After a few moments, he asked, "Aren't you going to say anything?"

What could I say? How do you respond to a comment like that? So I turned to face him, took an old British aristocratic stance, and bowed my best toward him.

"Thank you," I said and decided to go in and eat and not wait for my friend.

The irony of this story was that I had a major crush on Tony's brother. I didn't know it was a crush, I just thought I was interested in him as a person, but after that moment, I knew it for what it was.

I may have been sheltered in Lander—now Riverton, Wyoming, but I knew what a faggot was—and now I knew it was me. After that day, I started falling apart at school. I started acting up, skipping class, goofing off, and I just stopped worrying about what my teachers thought of me. My attitude went from being one of the better attitudes in the school to being one of the worst. After that first semester, I was asked to leave the school indefinitely until I could get my act together.

As an encore, I was kicked off the bus on the way back to Wyoming for bringing a Coke on board. They sure did set the bar low for rebellion.

The next few years were turbulent. I was still stinging from Tony's poisonous bite and feared being physically hurt because of my sexuality.

For those keeping score, we moved from Lander to Ft. Washakie and then from Ft. Washakie to Riverton—on Adams Street. It was while living on Adams that I went to Campion. This brings the total to 14.

By this time, my family had moved to Riverton, Wyoming, and Roger had left his job as a Bible salesman and was working for himself as a contractor. I still hated working with him, but since I wasn't in school anymore, there was no way he would let me lie around and do nothing. I was now spending much more time with him than I could handle. That also affected my psychological state.

During this time, I also discovered alcohol and drugs, specifically pot and speed. For the next few years, they would be my best friends. I was a speed freak and bordering on alcoholic. There was hardly a day that I wasn't drunk and on something. My favorite type of speed was the Black Beauty, but I also did Cross-tops, Yellow-jackets, Pink-hearts, Christmas trees—whatever I could get my hands on.

I have struggled with the symptoms of depression all my life (even though I never knew it), and at this point in my life, as I look back, I can see that those symptoms were pronounced. I couldn't even get out of bed most mornings, but speed helped me. I could set the alarm twenty minutes early, turn over, pop a pill, lie back in bed, and wait for the pill to take effect. Then at night, I could drink until I couldn't stand up and pass out somewhere until it was time to go home and start the routine all over again. Whatever I needed to feel, there were chemicals for that.

Needless to say, things in the family were difficult. While I may have been struggling with depression (it was diagnosed much later by my first therapist and confirmed by every therapist after that), thanks to the speed and the alcohol, I was now adding some serious mental and physical disorders to the list. The two most significant were paranoia and drug-induced schizophrenia. On the part of the paranoia, I lived in constant terror that someone would find out that I didn't like women (or that I was taking drugs, for that matter). While on the drugs, I could have radical mood swings and sometimes get violent. I never hurt anyone physically, but I could hurt them with words. I regretted it afterward, but I could never take them back.

At that time, Roger got the great idea that he would send me to a foster home where I could be out of his way. He and my mom fought bitterly over that, but my mom and I weren't getting along either. I blamed her for my troubles. It was her fault for marrying Roger, whom I hated. She let Roger move us to Wyoming, and she had to be why I was gay. I never told her any of this, but I felt that way and would do anything to get out of the house. I was desperate to be away from both her and Roger.

The first guy I ever told about my sexuality was someone I didn't tell about my sexuality. I met Mitch, and somehow, we became friends. He was just a year or two older than me, and I looked up to him. Literally: He was taller than me. He was tall and thin, had curly blonde hair, and would sit and listen to me talk about anything. One night while we were talking, he looked over at me and said, "I know." Then he added, "And it's okay." I knew what he was talking about but didn't say anything, not wanting to risk our friendship. A few weeks later, Mitch and I were visiting his mother and sister. That night Mitch's sister and her friend went out, and Mitch and I stayed home to watch his sister's kids. The kids were asleep, and we were in the kitchen. I was sitting on the counter smoking a cigarette, and he was standing in front of me. I blew smoke, and he accused me of blowing smoke in his face (in my high school, when you blew smoke in someone's face, that meant that you wanted to have sex with them).

"I didn't do it on purpose," I defended myself.

Mitch leaned in and kissed me. That was my first kiss ever by a man. My heart was racing, my blood was boiling, and I was in another world. It was the most powerful feeling I had ever felt up to then. I couldn't even talk. My mouth was so dry, my tongue swelled, and I wouldn't move. I've never been to heaven, but this had to be close.

That night when we went to bed, Mitch wrapped his leg around me and lay over my chest. My mouth was now arid, and I still couldn't talk. I was breathing like a man who had just run a race. I felt like I was in a dream, the best I had ever had (even better than the John Travolta dream).

However, things with Mitch were short-lived. Without explanation, he started treating me harshly, ignoring me, and showing me all the girls he was sleeping with. I had gone from being ecstatic to almost inconsolable in just a matter of weeks. What made this even more difficult was that I couldn't talk to anyone about it. Nobody knew what Mitch and I had been doing, and I didn't dare tell anyone. So I did my grieving all by myself with help from my friend Jack Daniels and some Coke. Nobody could even tell me how to get through such an experience.

As I began to realize I was gay, I did just that—I *realized*. I didn't decide to fall in love with John Travolta. I was innocently watching a movie when I found myself drawn to him like my friends were drawn to Olivia Newton-John. When I had those dreams that boys that age get, instead of involving women, mine involved men.

Homosexuality isn't a choice; it's a discovery. In the same way heterosexuality is a discovery. A young boy one day discovers that girls' breasts make weird things happen to him in the pit of his stomach. A young girl suddenly finds that she's drawn to a boy because of his looks and finds herself seeking a physical connection. These are discoveries, and healthy parents don't fault their kids for having these feelings. It's just like growing breasts. Girls don't choose to grow breasts; they just grow breasts. None of us chose to be sexual; we are sexual. It's built into us.

The same is true with the gay boy or girl. The boy discovers that the look and feel of another boy causes him to feel funny inside and finds himself aroused. The girl sees another girl and wants to be close and intimate, but another realization goes along with these discoveries. Unlike their counterparts who can express their feelings to their friends and, in some cases, their parents, gays, and lesbians can't because of the fear of retribution.

Let's look at another aspect of choice. For this, I will use the example of a computer as my analogy. Computers work on two basic principles: computer hardware and computer software. Computer hardware is the computer itself. The hard drive, the box it comes in, the processor, the chip, the wiring. On a computer, those things cannot be changed. Then there's the software. The software is what runs the computer, like the operating system, a word processor, and a graphics program. All these things help the computer do its work, and they can be added or removed as the user feels the need.

So how does this work in real life? Well, let's look at our hard drive. We have our height, eye color, hair color, genetic makeup, and gender. We cannot change these things (with a few exceptions). This is our hard drive.

What is our software? Our beliefs change from day to day, year to year. We can change where we live (I've done that a lot), what clothes we wear, who we choose to associate with, what we eat, and how much we eat. All these are choices we can make. This is our software. In other words, our religious beliefs are software; our sexuality is hardware.

No matter how much I want to, I will never be able to grow another inch. I can change my hair color, but only through dyes and bleaches, and always the true color will find its way through no matter how I try to change that. That's the nature of things. That's the hardware.

Here's an example of how it works. Suppose I told you to stop being straight. Or suppose I told you to have a homosexual affair? Suppose I told you to have sex with someone of the same gender just once. Could you? Most people couldn't. It would be going against their hardware, and they couldn't make themselves do it even on a one-time basis.

LOVE IN TRACTION

After Campion, a "relationship" with God was the last thing on my mind. I came home to Riverton, angry from the experience. I was angry at everybody: God, the Adventist Church, my parents, and the world. I tried to fit in with those around me, but I didn't fit in, and before long, I had been through three high schools (two of them religious). I was troubled at this point in my life. I was trying to run away from myself even though I didn't know that, and the problem was—wherever I went—there I was. I just kept on tagging along.

God was starting to look a lot like my father figures. He was cold and aloof and always played power games with me. There was no pleasing him. He demanded respect, but he was unwilling to earn that respect. God cursed me and then blamed me for it. Despite everything I had done to serve him, God did not care. He pushed, insulted, mistreated, and treated me like some insect that small boys torture and hurt before they finally step on them.

Hell no longer scared me at this point. I was so angry with God that the thought of spending eternity with him was almost unbearable. I hated God so much that I wanted nothing to do with him. Eternity with this God would be Hell. The God I saw in the Bible was pretty much an alcoholic father. When he was sober, he was loving and good to Israel, but when he was drunk, it was locusts, plagues, and brutal devastation.

I eventually ended up in an alternative high school geared toward students who didn't do well in the formal educational system. At least there, I could pretend that I was in school, and I did attend most of my classes most of the time. Granted, I wasn't always sober, but I was there and wasn't totally misbehaving either, so nobody bothered me. I think deep down inside, the teachers were hoping that I would make it, so they took it easy on me.

After a few months in the alternative school, I asked if I could attend a mainstream high school. They agreed. As I was sitting with the high school counselor, trying to figure out what classes I needed to take, he decided to put me into Speech and Drama. I needed some English, and he thought these classes would be easy for me. This event would be what Carl Jung would have called synchronicity. Two things happened in speech and drama. I found people that could handle me as I was without any judgment (aside from the typical high school "drama"). They didn't have a problem with my orientation (even though I was still cautious about what I said). For the first time, I could talk more openly about what was personal. The second point was that I found something I was good at and something that I loved doing. I started competing in oratory speech and humorous interpretation and was placed at speech meets.

This spilled over into other areas of school. For example, I had to keep my grade point average at a certain level and meet certain attendance criteria. Because of that, I started attending classes regularly and kept my grades above a C. My teachers were a big help as well. They were amazing. I was surprised at how far out of their way they would go to ensure I was eligible to compete.

My science class just happened to start immediately after lunch. This was hard to make because I was usually goofing around at lunch. I would try to get to class before the bell, but I was often late. Rather than punish me by knocking my grade down or counting me absent, my science teacher had me write a one-thousand-word essay detailing why I wouldn't be late to "a movie," to "catch an airplane," or "to Mr. Tucker's class." So I wrote the article, feeling very much the smartass. The article had a recurring theme and read like a comedy routine. He liked it and told my other teachers about it.

I struggled in English class because I missed a couple of assignments. My English teacher, Mrs. Heller, asked me during class to get a copy of this article I had written for Mr. Tucker. I did, and she read it. I heard her laughing as she did, and at the end of class, she graded it and handed it back to me. This brought my grade up one point so that I could still compete in the following speech meet.

Still, I was struggling to get to class on time. Again, after lunch—I had to report to the front office and get a pass so I could go down the hall to my class. Mrs. Smyth was wondering why she should give me this pass and asked why I was late.

"I had a flat tire," I told her.

"That's the fourth flat tire you've had this week," she retorted.

I thought for a minute, then looked her dead in the eye and said, "Well, they're all fixed now."

She looked me dead in the eye too. We stood there for a minute looking at each other, and I swear I saw a twinkle in her eye and what looked like a grin start to spread itself across her face.

"Then I guess you won't have any more flat tires," she finally said, writing out my pass.

Another day, after lunch, I was running to class. I was cutting it close, and I would make it if I ran. There were several of us all late and running. The principal was in the hallway and saw us, and immediately yelled— "walk!" We all slowed down. He saw me and announced, "You can run." Run, I did. I made it to class just as the second bell rang.

During that time, my best friend's stepmom's dad died (I couldn't think of any other way to say it). I remember we were over at the house, and she talked about it. That's when I told her about my brother, Brian. As I talked casually about the event, I was drawn back to the time that it happened. I remembered all the guilt and harsh words I had spoken. I remembered the fights and the competition between us for attention. Then I remembered the day I visited him at the funeral home. I'll never forget seeing his body lying in the casket. I tried so hard at eleven years old to understand why he couldn't open his eyes and talk to me. His body was there just as I remembered it, but "he" was gone, and I couldn't figure out where he went or why God would take him away (I was especially troubled that God would take Brian away but leave his body). That seemed cruel to me at the time.

The wound opened up, and the toxin poured out. I released the guilt, the anger with God, that sense of abandonment, and I recalled the memory of his little body laying cold in the casket and wishing I could hold him there and comfort him. For the first time in my life, I talked about it. At seventeen, six years after the event, I had finally opened up to someone.

Through this process of opening up and talking about my feelings with my friends and feeling like I was good at something like speech, I started letting go of the drugs and alcohol. I remember taking four Black Beauties one night, and I thought I had overdosed. As the night went on, I started to feel sharp pains in my chest, and I thought I was going to die. I thought I would stand in front of God, and we would finally have it out. I wasn't sure if I was quite ready for that altercation just yet.

I was hanging out at the local teen hang-out, the Riverton Roller Ranch. As you might have guessed, this was a roller-skating rink. Roller skating was popular in the eighties, even in Riverton. As the night went on, I started to feel the overwhelming effect of the drugs, and I could hardly breathe. Every breath felt labored as if I was struggling to fill my lungs with air. I was worried. My body went numb. I kept moving to keep my mind off the terror that was actually making the whole situation worse.

Then something else happened. There were some guys there who wanted to beat the hell out of me for whatever reason (and I think we know what reason that was). The next thing I knew, one of my friends took me by the arm and escorted me out of the building quickly and quietly. We got in his car, and he drove me away. I was shaking and couldn't concentrate, and because of my altered state, I wasn't clear on what was happening. My friend wondered if he shouldn't take me to the hospital, but to go there would be to admit that I had taken an illegal substance, and that was an even greater risk. So we drove around until the speed wore off, which it eventually did hours later.

I decided I wasn't willing to go through something like that again, and from that moment on, my love affair with speed was over. I'd figure out my own damn way to get out of bed, thank you very much. I still liked to drink and couldn't imagine a life without pot, but the speed was gone.

This also became noticeable to my teachers. They could see that I was more coherent and less strung out. I stopped hanging out at the "fence" during lunch (the fence is where we all hung out to smoke and take pleasure in other illegal chemicals). As a result, I noticed a change in my relationship with them (my teachers). I had always had the vague suspicion that they were somehow trying to help me, but with the fog gone, I could see it. I started having fun in school and expressing myself even more.

Even though things were better for me now, I was still the lone gay man in a small town that didn't understand or appreciate homosexuality. As I look back on my time in Riverton, I realize that Riverton itself wasn't against me; only a certain few had a problem with it, but those certain few made things the most difficult. I had some good friends who knew the truth about me and were willing and able to accept me as a friend. Showing up at parties could be dangerous, even if I was invited. I remember one such party. It was a bonfire/school party (unsanctioned by the authorities), and many people were there. I went with other friends, but we had to leave quickly because some people there weren't happy to see us. As I walked away, someone threw a beer bottle at my head. It missed, but it scared me, nonetheless.

I was also asked to leave a few places and told I wasn't welcome there anymore. I'll never forget the first time that happened. My sister and I had been partying with these friends for years. One night we went to hang out, and Ted, the guy dating the girl who rented the apartment, turned on me. He stood in the middle of the living room and announced that I wasn't welcome in their home and needed to leave. Of course, he told Rachel she could stay, but she was loyal, and we both left.

For years I never knew why he had turned on me like that. Was I out of control? Did I not buy enough alcohol? Was I over there too often? Ironically, the obvious never occurred to me. It wasn't until many years later that Rachel found out that he had heard that I might be gay. It was a rumor, completely unconfirmed.

Despite the emotional healing I experienced over Brian, I was still angry with God. Why would he even consider bringing such a plague on me? Someone had something derisive and vicious to say at every turn.

It was about this time that the AIDS epidemic broke; only then it was announced as "a new cancer in homosexual men." You guessed it; every Christian I knew viewed this as God's judgment on homosexuality. Sodom and Gomorrah were finally being judged, and I listened to the Christians in our town sing with glee the story of God's coming judgment. They truly felt that it was about time God did something about this scourge.

I felt like I needed to get even with God for what he was doing to me, so I turned to the one person/entity I knew could hurt him. I tried (literally) to sell my Soul to Satan. I did the spells and incantations, spilled my blood in the middle of the pentagram, drew up a legal contract, and signed it with my blood. I wanted fame, fortune, and male lovers galore, and I figured Satan would bring them to me. I assumed he'd do anything to get a Soul away from God. I knew that I faced the peril of burning in hell, but I still had enough of the Adventist teaching in me to make it worth the risk. I figured I would burn for a while, and then it would be over, and I would be gone forever. I didn't care about that. After all, I hated God; why would I want to spend eternity with him and his Homo-Hatin ways?

So this was my opportunity: my window, the one way I could get even with God. But it never took. I never saw or felt Satan, and no demon entered the room. I put a key in Daniel 7—nothing. (According to my pastors, that was supposed to call the devil.) I said the Lord's Prayer backward—nothing. I had heard all the stories in church about demons attacking people who played with Ouija Boards, and yet here I was, deliberately calling them, and there was no answer. I kept trying to fine-tune my approach. Maybe I had the wrong number, or I needed more blood (or less blood), or if I said every other word of the Lord's Prayer backward or became a Democrat: but there was no Satan. Talk about depressing. Even Satan didn't want me.

I had friends who believed they were witches and warlocks, and they told me that they had become frightened of me because I had so much "power," but the reality was; the only power I had was anger, just like Darth Vader: and it was that anger that frightened them and everyone around me.

NOT SO HOT IN CLEVELAND

I met Eddie in my last year of church school in Lander when his parents heard about the church and entered him and his younger sister. We became instant friends and stayed friends for many years until I went to Campion. We both had a lot in common. Violent fathers, dysfunctional families—and we were both gay. Only we didn't know that last part about each other. Or at least not consciously.

Eddie lived with his father and stepmom, just opposite my parental situation. His father was also verbally, physically, and emotionally violent and abusive. His stepmom was a drama queen. She could put any one of the television "Real Housewives" to shame. One day, because she wasn't getting enough attention, she took a small knife and stabbed herself in the chest, right around the heart. She was cautious not to do any actual damage; she just wanted us to notice her and feel sorry for her. Eddie was embarrassed, but he could talk about it with me.

Later, she would—probably for attention—start a rumor about her son and another boy who also attended the school. Because she was only trying to get attention, she was careful not to push it too far, which left that question in everybody's mind. I couldn't help but wonder what it must have been like for Eddie to have parents like this.

Eddie was also a diabetic and heavily reliant on insulin. I remember his parents showing up at our door one evening, feigning fear because he was missing. They told us that Eddie had started a fight, and they told him to go to his room and that he snuck out. They didn't realize this until later when they brought dinner to his room.

While they were desperately seeking sympathy, I snuck out of the house and made my way to the park, where Eddie and I hung out often. He was there. His story was similar, but there were some glaring differences. First, there was a fight over what I don't even remember. He got violent with Eddie, and Eddie left, more for his protection.

We determined that Eddie would return home, call our house, and let everyone know he was okay. And then I snuck back into the house.

After our graduation, I was shipped to Loveland, Colorado, for my first year in high school. While I was there, Eddie contacted his real mom, who lived in Lakewood, OH (a suburb just west of Cleveland on the lake). He wanted out of his situation so fiercely, and she told him to come and live with her and her husband, a doctor at the Cleveland Clinic.

We kept in touch via phone, cards, and letters. Since we were in the early 80s, the very idea of electronic mail was just a concept in something called the ARPANET, and nobody had yet considered any other uses for it other than the military.

Because of the distance, we opened up to each other through our correspondence. When I returned from Colorado, our mutual friend began to broker a treaty between us that she would nurture. She and Eddie were so close that he felt safe telling her everything about him. That he was gay. Ronda was also my best friend, and I felt I could tell her anything, but I couldn't tell her I was gay. I could not come out and say it... not even to myself. So I pretended I hated gay people and always acted disgusted when people talked about it.

So with Eddie's permission, she took me for a drive and told me what she and Eddie had discussed.

Weirdly enough, I wasn't surprised. I already thought he was based on his mannerisms. I wasn't upset and used this as an opportunity to come out to somebody finally... Ronda. And then to Eddie. Finally, since that day in Campion, I could talk about this.

Eddie invited me to come out and visit, and I started giving it serious thought. Cleveland would be perfect for me. I could go out there, find a job as a DJ (that's what I did in Riverton), and find that man who would complete my life. Then I would become famous, and my life would be so wonderful. I'd take over for Rick Dees and become a rock star, only to move on to make my mark acting in movies.

As coincidence—or fate would have it, a high school friend of mine, Mark, stopped by to tell me that he was on his way to Chillicothe, Ohio, and if I wanted to ride along with him, I could split the gas, and that would get me as far as Columbus, Ohio. From there, I could take a bus to Cleveland. That was the perfect plan. I would go to Cleveland, find my Prince Charming, who loved me and wanted to take care of me and live happily ever after. I would never look back on Riverton.

There's something kind of obnoxious about fantasy. It never plays out in real life as it does in our heads. Cleveland didn't turn out like I had hoped it would. Of course, looking back, I realize it had a lot to do with my immaturity and inability to separate fantasy from reality. However, it was still tricky for me... not to mention an eye-opener.

I hadn't dated in Riverton (men) for obvious reasons. I had three girlfriends in high school, and they were sweet, but I couldn't give them what they wanted. My first girlfriend, Candice, was cute and spunky, and I liked her. But no matter how long I was with her, the most we ever did was lie on the couch cuddling. She was upset because we were alone all night, and I never touched her breasts. Needless to say, she broke up with me.

Judy was a cute blonde girl whom I went to school with. While I was dating her, her older sister Josephine started experimenting with a lesbian. Josephine told me about it and asked me what I thought. I was still pretending to be straight then, so she wasn't sure how I would handle it. It was weird to me. I couldn't imagine anyone having sex with a girl, let alone a girl with another girl. In my mind, two girls having sex with each other was double the gross, double the yuck.

After Judy, I dated Jill. I even took her to the prom. Later that night, at a party, after I had a lot to drink, I decided that I could have sex with her. I looked over at her and told her just that. She was ready, and before I could say anything else, she had me by the hand and had taken me to another room. Granted, this was sex, and sex should be much fun no matter who you're with—but when it came down to it, I wasn't into it. She had to tell me what to do the whole time because I didn't know. For example, I was interested in her breasts but not how a straight man would be. They were like pillows, which I batted around like a cat bathed a ball of yarn. Still, it was good for her because whatever she told me to do, I did it.

So my dating skills could have been improved. As a result of not dating and because I had never been away from home, I wasn't prepared to deal with the realities of real life, authentic life, all by myself. My first encounter, Mitch, was the only guy I had ever "known," which was a fiasco. So I had no idea what a relationship was like (outside of my parents, and that's not much to go on). This lack of knowledge made the fantasies more believable but didn't prepare me for the disillusion.

When I arrived in Cleveland, I found I took to the city. Instead of being afraid, having come from such a small town, I blended in. I was at home downtown. I barely thought about the crowds, the congestion, the traffic. I enjoyed it. This was proof I was in the 'big city.' It was the biggest city I had been in so far, the second biggest city, Casper, Wy., between thirty and forty thousand when I lived in the state.

Cleveland had bars that were dedicated to gay people. They were called gay bars, and though I was only 18, a little makeup and a fake ID got me in the door. It was like another world. There were men around me everywhere—men who, like me, wanted to have sex with other men. Almost every man in these bars shared my sexuality.

Yet, as most of you know, gay and straight people who hang out in bars don't necessarily make for great dates. There are many games played in those establishments.

On one of my first nights there, I met Mark. Mark was at the bar with his friend Kyle, and I thought Kyle was gorgeous. However, Mark talked to me and hung out with me. So at the end of the night, when Mark asked me to go home with him, I did. However, it turned out that Mark was spending the night at Kyle and Jerry's house. Kyle was dating Jerry, and they were living together. Jerry was out of town for the weekend, however.

A short while after I arrived at the house, it was apparent I was into Kyle. Since I had never done this before, I didn't realize how I acted or the signals I sent out. But Kyle was also into me, and he started kissing me and making out.

Mark was pissed. As a teenager, with all my focus on me, and hormones running amok, I didn't necessarily try to hide my joy and being manhandled. So Mark stormed out of the house angrily, calling me an asshole as he did.

I've had decades to go over that night and realize that even at the moment, my very first openly gay encounter, I had taken on the person and immersed myself in the drama. I was, indeed, an asshole. Still, I was naïve and stupid.

The only thing Kyle and I ever did was make out that night, and then Eddie picked me up the next day, and we went to Cedar Point, an amusement park, to play for the rest of the day. Regardless of how much fun I was having, my mind was on Kyle. He might be the man I was looking for.

So I called him that night, hoping we could set up a date. However, I discovered two things during that conversation. Kyle was drunk the night I went to his house, and today, he was sober, meaning that his feelings about our night together were different. There was no way he was going to leave his boyfriend.

And that was the best experience I had.

This was a rough game, and I wasn't equipped to play it. Not at all. As I said, until you date, you have no idea what's involved in dating. There's a lot of rejection, vulnerability, and confused emotion... and that's in a healthy relationship. Since I wasn't aware of that at the time, these occurrences, one by one, only made me feel more isolated. Nothing was going the way I had envisioned in my fantasy. I couldn't even find a job as a DJ. There was a grocery store behind Eddie's house, and they were looking for a carryout, but I wanted to be a DJ, find a man, and get rich and famous—none of which I could do working at a grocery store.

So, as a result, when my friend Mark called me from Chillicothe to let me know that he was headed back to Riverton, I decided to go back with him.

My time in Cleveland had left some marks... scars, more like it. On the positive, I could be out, whereas I couldn't in Wyoming. But people play games, and gay men and women are no exception, and I was caught off guard when they started playing them with me (I was completely thrown off guard when I realized that I was playing them too). Because of my upbringing, I think, or because I wasn't willing to look at my experiences in Cleveland honestly, I thought that the games and how people behaved were just a sign from God that homosexuality was wrong, just like everybody had been saying. After all, if you can't succeed in a homosexual relationship, that is a sign that God doesn't sanction homosexual relationships. Of course, most of the Christians I know have been married at least twice, so by that argument, you could say that relationships, in general, aren't sanctioned by God (and sometimes I wonder).

Another downside of the Cleveland experience was that I became a bit of a flamer (That's like saying the Pope is a bit Catholic). I developed the "lisp," the "swish," the "pitch," and boy could I play the Diva. These characteristics would not play well in Riverton, so when I got home, I had to be extremely careful to say as little as I could, avoid moving too much, and sit with my legs uncrossed and my feet flat on the floor.

I still had one "official" year of high school. When I went to Cleveland, I did not intend to finish high school (why would a famous DJ need to finish high school?). But I was at least two years behind in credits (from being kicked out of school so many times), and it just seemed like too much work getting caught up. Still, all my friends were in school, so I decided I might as well finish. There should be one thing in life I finished, and school might as well be it. I took four or five classes as home study courses on top of my regular classes to graduate in 1984 (technically, only one year later than I should have graduated). I lost my heart for speech and drama and no longer felt like competing. Part of that may have been my disillusionment in Cleveland, but I also think that part of it was that I never felt supported by my speech and drama teacher, and I didn't want to go through all this competition again without someone who had my back.

Once in school, to get myself to where I could interact with my fellow students without looking like Jack McFarland from Will and Grace (only not nearly as funny), I watched several of the jocks around school, and I used their movements and motions to teach me how to "look straight." This was a little difficult since the jocks didn't like being looked at, especially by a faggot. It was one of the main reasons I skipped gym during my first year back in Campion. So I was careful. I learned to rely on my peripheral vision. I could watch them without "watching" them, and it helped. It wasn't long before I was "straight acting." This took a lot of pressure off of me during my last school year, and the harassment went down.

FOCUS ON YOUR OWN DAMN FAMILY

At home, things were starting to unravel. Our family dysfunction had reached epic proportions even for the state of Wyoming. My younger sister had been dating a semi-professional wrestler (the ones on TV who like to throw chairs), and she ran away to Phoenix with him. Roger was becoming more violent, and I was drinking way too much. Roger was still an elder in the Church and sure knew how to keep up appearances. At church, he was the model of a good Christian, but at home, he was violent and abusive.

One day Roger and I had an especially gruesome altercation. Roger's way of dealing with me was through violence. If I pissed him off (which wasn't hard to do), then he threw punches. This particular day he picked me up and threw me across the kitchen. I was so angry that I grabbed a sharp knife. This freaked out everybody, and suddenly there was much screaming. I knew I had gone too far, but now I didn't know how to get out of it. So I stood there while he tried to distract me. I wasn't distracted, but I wasn't going to stab him either. So I braced myself.

He grabbed the knife, and the next thing I knew, he attacked me like a crazed grizzly bear. I managed to get out of his grasp, and I took off. I ran out of the house and into town to get away. I didn't want to tell any of my friends, so I just wandered the streets of Riverton for several hours. My mom eventually found me and drove me home.

Ultimately, the family was turned over to the state of Wyoming. Roger was so good at getting people to sympathize with him that the state thought that he and his two daughters were victims of me. Roger weighed at least two-hundred-fifty pounds, and he used to work out, so there were residual muscles (although he was still fat), and he was strong. At five-foot-eleven and-a-half, I weighed in at one-hundred-fifty pounds soaking wet with a heavy leather jacket, kneepads, and hiking boots. I was so skinny that if I turned sideways and stuck out my tongue, I looked like a zipper, but somehow, I terrorized this colossal man. Granted, I was about four inches taller than him, but my only real physical advantage over him was that I could run fast when I was scared.

So I was brought into the social worker's office. It was just me and my mom on this particular day. Edward was the social worker's name, and he looked at me, somewhat confused, when I walked through the door. I didn't know what to think, but I sat down and listened as he and my mom talked about the family situation. I didn't pay much attention to their conversation until Edward looked at me and said, "I hear that you're a dope-blowing drunk."

That took me by surprise. He was candid with me. I didn't know quite how to respond. So I looked him straight and said, "I used to be, but I've cleaned myself up."

We held each other's gaze for several seconds, and then he looked back at my mom, and they started talking again. It was agreed that my mom and Roger would start counseling. Edward told her that our problems (the kids) were actually their problems (my mom and Roger) and that the kids would be just fine as soon as they got their lives together.

Roger only made two counseling sessions, and then he never returned. Meanwhile, my mom was making strides in her therapy. Meanwhile, my sister had been found and remanded to the state of Wyoming, where she spent a few months in a girl's detention home. Once she was out, her case would again go to court, where a judge would decide who would have parental custody. She wanted to go and live with her father, and the courts would decide if that was possible.

Edward came to the house to visit and check up on the family. Edward and I were getting along splendidly by this time. It turned out that we liked each other. He would often tell me that Roger and I didn't get along because I was much older emotionally. I liked hearing that. He also told me why he had given me such a confused look the first time we met. It turns out that the way Roger had talked, he had the impression that I must have been about six-foot-ten, four hundred pounds, with arms hanging down to my knees, not this skinny kid whose only chance for survival in a fight would be to run like hell.

As we were touring the house, Edward noticed a large hole in the wall at the top of the stairs. He asked me about it, and I said, "That's where Roger threw me up the stairs." Later he noticed a hole in the wall at the bottom of the stairs. He asked me about that, and I said, "That's where Roger threw me down the stairs." Then there was the hole in the family room, the hole by my bedroom, some pieces of the kitchen cabinet broken away... all results of fights between me and Roger.

When the family's situation was brought before the courts of Wyoming, and Edward testified regarding our situation, it was not a big surprise that he didn't have a lot of good things to say regarding the whole mess. Oddly enough, though, he had very little to say about me. By the time it was over, my sister had been sent to live in Montana with her father, and the rest of the family was stinging from Edward's assessment. Roger was livid; it was all he could talk about for weeks. I steered clear of Roger during that time because I wasn't interested in adding more holes to the house's walls.

In the meantime, my mother had decided that if she and Roger were going to work things out, they would have to do it separately. So she separated from him. I should have been excited when she told me this, but I wasn't. I was terrified. My sister would be leaving Riverton in just a few days to live with her father, and it would be me and my mother. Just the two of us, and I still had one year of high school to finish.

All this brought me to that night in September 1984.

LOVE IN AUCTION

Now that I knew that God wanted me, if I were going to stay with Him, I would somehow have to reorient my sexual identity. After my mom left Roger, I approached Edward (who also was a therapist) and asked him to counsel me and help me change. He was reluctant to do so because he didn't feel it was ethically correct, but I insisted. I told Edward I wanted to serve God my whole life and didn't want anything coming between us. Edward told me that my explanation made him feel "okay" about counseling me (I should point out that Edward was an atheist). I think he also thought that counseling would be good for me, and if nothing else, we could work some of my other stuff out.

During my remaining years in Riverton, I continued to see Edward. It was doing wonders for many of my family issues, but it wasn't helping regarding my sexual identity. No matter how we talked or how much time I spent with him, my orientation wasn't changing even slightly. Every cute boy I saw would suddenly steal my attention away from whatever I was doing at the time. Still, Edward was able to teach me about emotional maturity. He taught me emotions were simply feedback, showing me what was happening inside. They were energy in motion: E(energy)=Motion. He taught me how to use my emotions and let them work for me. He helped me accept that all my emotions, including anger, were okay. I think Edward, under the guise of counseling me on my sexuality, gave me so much more than that.

Shortly after I stopped seeing Edward, one event discouraged me to such a degree that it took me days to come out of it. Looking back, it's rather funny, but it sent me into an emotional tailspin at the time.

The most profound part of this "tragedy" was that it happened while I was reading the Bible. I was reading the gospel of Mark. Mark mentioned a Roman soldier. It was that simple: A generic Roman soldier. A sudden visual flashed in my mind, and I pictured a Roman soldier in his mini-skirt. I could see his strong legs, mighty thighs, muscular chest, and gorgeous face. He was strong and in control—and all man—all sexy and gorgeous man.

I was overcome with tortured anguish at that moment. I realize that's a lot of hyperbole, but it was a dark time.

"God?" I shouted into my pillow. "How can I overcome this when even the Bible gets me sexually aroused?" I couldn't believe it. The book that was supposed to set me free was making things worse. It was a moment of such utter hopelessness that I decided I wouldn't make it.

Of course, now that I'm on the other side of it, I've turned it into a rather amusing story that goes something like this:

> I felt as if I was doomed forever and I'd never be free, so I cried out to God, "I can't take it anymore! If this is to be what it's like for the rest of my life, then I don't want to be here. Let's finish it now; let's not drag it on!"
>
> Then I felt something well up deep in my soul. It was laughter. God was laughing. It was a deep laugh that seemed to come from everywhere. I felt it in the air around me, in the ground below me, in the sky above me, and, most disconcertingly, I felt it deep inside of me.
>
> It was a deep laugh filled with irony, tinged with satire, and shaded with a deep sense of paradox.
>
> "This isn't funny, God!" I shouted when I got over the shock.
>
> Then I heard a voice deep within my soul, steeped with compassion.
>
> "Precious child," the voice chortled. "I know you—intimately. I know one of the trillions of cells that make up your body. I know the ground you walk on and the Earth that bears you up. I know every atom of the Universe you call home and every

star that shines over your head. I know the solar systems and galaxies you live among, and I know funny... and that was funny!"

Of course, I laugh about it now, but there was something intensely hopeless at the time. Even something that was supposed to give me hope, like the Bible, was being used against me. As I said, it took me several days to pull out of the depression that followed that event.

On the upside, my songwriting abilities were taking off. My songs were getting more sophisticated. Suffering makes for great music. My songs contained a heartfelt desire to connect with God at the level of my Soul. The lyrics were a sincere cry for him, to be like him, to be near him. I started to write plays and sketches, and short stories. Much of this was Edward's idea. He thought I could help myself by writing about my feelings and struggles in a way that was rewarding for me. He had me write my feelings in play form and do monologues from the perspective of my angry self and my frightened self. So write I did.

I remember one day playing one of my songs for some friends who had come for a visit. I sang them a song I had just finished. The title of this song was "In Your Arms (It's Alright)." The song talked about my fears and struggles but then went into the chorus, "When you hold me in your arms, it's all right." It was a love song between me and God. When I finished with the song and looked around, there were tears. They were crying.

Events like this caused me to believe that God was with me and that he genuinely was accepting me, and that he would bless me as a professional singer/songwriter... eventually... but I had to become straight first. I knew deep down inside that I would never get to be the professional status (which was my greatest dream then) until I dealt with my sexuality (and became straight), and every day I prayed, pleaded, and cajoled God to help me find that way out.

Part of my journey back to God involved going back to church. Since the only church I knew was the Seventh-day Adventist church, that's where I returned, but it was not a happy homecoming. I had discovered Christian rock by now, so I was even more committed to my African beat than ever. I also knew there was no way I would be able to make that much of a sacrifice. I would have to subject myself to giving up my bacon cheeseburgers, diet coke, and cartoons on Saturdays, so after only a few weeks, I realized that particular philosophy wasn't for me.

I made friends occasionally and attended a church or two, but quite frankly, I was bothered by what I saw. The churches were varied but not healthy. One Foursquare church I attended was so austere that it made the Seventh-day Adventist church look like a party church. This pastor made his congregants submit to all kinds of personal intrusions into their personal life so that they would remain holy (by his standards). He led his congregation by telling them exactly how to live every moment of their lives. He tried that with me, but I was fresh out of the "rebellion" scene, sex, drugs, and rock and roll. There was still plenty of rebellion in me, and in this case, rebellion may have saved me.

Another church I tried out was so into the emotional thing that it made your everyday charismatic look mellow. They took it to a whole new level.

I tried out a church led by a former pimp. He even had a pimp's name. None of us knew it then, but while he was leading this fledgling congregation, he was still working the streets of Riverton (there was prostitution in a small town like Riverton?).

One day I went to church with a friend, and they had a guest pastor. This pastor tried to guilt the young people in the congregation and mainly wanted to communicate how evil Rock and Roll music was. I had heard this line from the Seventh-day Adventist church so often that I was bored. You all know the arguments. Jimmy Page and Robert Plant were in a hypnotic trance when they wrote Stairway to Heaven, they were disciples of Anton LeVey, and their songs were backward masked (Satan my Satan 666).

He also told the story of the missionaries in Africa whose kids were playing their Christian rock music and then were informed by the people of the village that it was the same beat that they used to call the devil. Then he called for us to bring our rock and roll records and tapes (and yes, 8-tracks) to have a good ol' fashioned record burning.

I was annoyed. This was a message I had heard so many times that I didn't want to hear it anymore, so I got up to leave. The moment I did, the pastor instructed the other church members to try and stop me. They all did. They stood up and tried to surround me, and at that point, I ran as quickly as I could out the door with other members trying to catch me.

The next church I attended was hit with the rather salacious news that their pastor was "addicted" to pornography. He was caught buying pornographic magazines at a local magazine store.

Needless to say, I gave up on finding a church. I was still a Christian, but I found solace in my music and writing. They were my church until I left Riverton.

During that period, I met two girls, and both had a crush on me. I liked them, too, so I tried dating. The first girl I met was Josie. We were both musicians. She played the flute, and I played the piano. We would play together from time to time, and we had a great time. Our friendship blossomed until it became evident that she wanted to go further than that.

The second girl I met was Tina. Tina was a singer, and she loved my music. I worked at a radio station then, doing a Christian show called *The Gospel Express*. This show aired every Sunday morning. I would play music and write comedy sketches for it. Tina would listen to my sketches before they aired and advise me on how to improve them if they needed improvement. I still remember her laughing so hard at one of my sketches that she nearly spit out her lunch while I was previewing it for her.

Eventually, I had to tell Josie and Tina what I was dealing with because they couldn't understand why I wouldn't have more physical contact with them—or why it was clumsy and insincere when we did have physical contact.

What's significant about this is the way these girls responded to me. Even in Riverton, Wyoming, with such a small exposure to this issue, literally every girl I "dated" took this news in stride and supported me. Of course, there were arguments, disagreements, and frustrations, but those were over many things, not just my sexuality. We all believed God would "heal" me and set me free. To that end, they were a constant support for me. I could express my frustration; I could talk openly.

As I look back, these people are important to me because they showed me that while I may have felt alone, the Universe was bringing people into my life who loved me—as me. Yes, they wanted to date and get close, but even when it became apparent that wouldn't happen, they hung around and stayed friends.

> *We moved from Ft Washakie to Riverton, on Adams Street. Then from Adams Street to the house that Roger built. Then when my moved left Roger, we moved into an apartment near the school. After graduation, we moved to another apartment. We moved to Cody, Wy, from this apartment—bringing the total of moves up to 17.*

After high school graduation, my mom was transferred with her job to Cody, Wyoming, and I decided that I would move with her. We moved to Cody, and my sexuality came with me. In Cody, I met some wonderful people (or they seemed wonderful at the time), and I soon found myself in a new church. It was a small group of people who met in a little wooden building. This congregation was the result of an earlier church split. I took to these people immediately, and we were always hanging out doing church things.

I met one lady in the church with a "healing" ministry. In other words, she counseled people and prayed with them. So I set up some time to talk with her. Edina was a wonderful friend too, and I could trust her. I trusted her with my story and her relationship with God to be sincere and honest.

After we had gotten to know one another, she did confide in me that she was afraid that I would seduce her sons but that she prayed about it, and God revealed to her that I was trustworthy and her sons would be safe. This wasn't the last time I would be confronted with this prejudice. Christians were led to believe that that's what we gays did; we seduced poor young boys and forced them to be gay. It's one of the most painful biases gay men experience: we're labeled pedophiles, even when that couldn't be further from the truth.

I was often frustrated with how the Christians I came in contact with somehow thought that gay people would fuck anybody without restraint. They believed that gays could "convert" others, which was somehow their goal. That's the homosexual agenda, to make everyone else gay. I'll never forget one man in particular. He was heavy-set (actually, he was just plain fat), he had greasy hair, missing teeth, and the IQ of a house plant (my apologies to houseplants). He lived in fear that the gays were going to get him. Because I've never been good at keeping my mouth shut, I finally asked him how it was he thought any self-respecting gay man would ever find him attractive. He was somewhat taken aback and offended, but he told me that that's what the gays do. They attack without discrimination. I wanted to tell him right then and there that I was a gay man, and I wouldn't touch him if he were the only thing standing between me and Jason Bateman's eternal love and devotion.

Now, when someone says that to me, I respond, "If you're afraid that there's someone or something out there that can somehow turn you gay... Congratulations! You're already gay." That ends the discussion pretty fast.

I spent a year with Edina, trying, if nothing else, to control things. Occasionally I had bad days when I just wanted to go out and find someone who would take me in their arms and hold me close and make love to me. I could talk to Edina about that; she understood without judgment. We talked a lot. We prayed a lot. We tried some role-playing. She even cast out several demons and unclean spirits out of me that she suspected to be playing a part in this stubborn malady. It was a pretty long list.

When I talk about this to people now, they're surprised that after all of this counseling, talking, and praying, something didn't shift. The best description of this struggle is this metaphor: take a beach ball, fill it with air, and then try to hold it underwater. No matter how hard you try, that beach ball is going to do everything it can to rise to the surface, and sooner or later, you're either going to have to pop it to keep it under the water, or you're going to have to give up and let it surface. You can only fight it until you become so exhausted that you either give up or drown.

Edina offered advice and taught me a lot about expecting from God rather than just begging him and hoping that I could catch him in a good mood (hell, I even saw her demand God on a couple of occasions). So I set out to "expect" God to help me go straight. It had an interesting effect on me. It didn't change how I felt about men, but it did make going through the experience a little easier, and from that time forward, in my relationship with God, I was less of a victim. In other words, I stopped viewing myself as a victim, even to God and started adding some personal responsibility.

Still, nothing changed around my sexuality.

Later that year, a guest pastor visited our church for special revival meetings. His favorite subject was the Devil. Every other sentence was about the Devil. I remember hearing him repeatedly relating how he laughed at the Devil. He laughed at the Devil once when... then there was the time... and so on. I was beginning to think that he and the Devil were in the middle of some codependent relationship.

One night after his sermon, he did a question-and-answer session where he took questions from the congregation. On this particular night, someone asked that age-old question, "What is the unpardonable sin?" Without hesitation, he said—and I quote, "homosexuality." That was it. That was the unpardonable sin. I could feel the blood run out of my face, and I just sat there, cold and dead. The logical part of me knew better, but still, there it was, a sense of despair washing over me.

Edina grabbed me immediately after the service and asked me how I was doing. I told her OK, but she had spent enough time with me to know better. She invited me to come over to the house immediately afterward to talk. She also invited several other people over on the pretense of having a get-together because she didn't want to draw attention to me in any way. As soon as everybody was mingling, she found a place to talk privately, and I started crying. I knew in my head that I hadn't committed the unpardonable sin. Still, I also felt in my heart that I would never be of any use to God until I got rid of this scourge, and while it might not have been the unpardonable sin, it was still significant, and there was no way out.

Later that year, I "felt a burden," as they say in Christianity, for suicide. Something stirred in me, and I started researching suicide. I can't honestly say if it was because I was struggling with those thoughts myself or if it was one of those instances where I was going to be able to step in and do some good to the Universe.

One night at a church Singles gathering, one of my friends, a nurse, was telling us about a young boy who had just been admitted to her hospital. He had tried to shoot himself in the heart, but the bullet missed, bounced off a bone somewhere in his chest, and, while it did damage, made its way out through the back without hitting the heart. He survived, but it was critical at first.

Something in me believed that was why I was experiencing that "calling." I went to the hospital and introduced myself. I was just barely twenty, and Calvin was starting high school. When I introduced myself, his mom was in the room, and she looked relieved that somebody was there for her son. She excused herself and left the room. Now it was just me and Calvin. It was uncomfortable at first, but I hung out, and we chatted some, and I promised him I would be there the next day—and I kept that promise.

After a few days, it was time for him to have the tubes removed that they had inserted to keep him alive. This was extremely painful for him, and I remember him in so much pain. Still, he was recovering.

After a few weeks, he was released from the hospital, and I would go over to his house, and we'd all play cards. I enjoyed spending time with Calvin and his family. I still look back on those moments fondly.

After he was well enough to travel, I took him to one of our youth meetings at the church I was attending. After the service, the pastor took Calvin aside and handed him a pamphlet detailing how killing yourself was a guaranteed trip straight to Hell. I was livid. I asked Calvin how he was doing... Calvin didn't talk much, especially about his feelings, and I wasn't comfortable pushing him, so I explained that the pastor was wrong. I knew that God would never punish someone because they felt they had no more options. That wasn't love to me. So I explained to Calvin that he would be fine and that it was between him and God, and nobody else had any say about it, not even a pastor.

Calvin didn't say much, but I continued to hang out with him, and when we were together, we had fun.

Later, Calvin's family decided to try out a Methodist or Lutheran church (I don't remember which). During the service, they partook of communion, which apparently is a no-no if you're not a member. That Sunday afternoon, the pastor drove out to their house to chastise them for participating in their communion since they weren't church members. I couldn't believe it. This poor kid couldn't get a break.

During this time, Rock Hudson finally succumbed to AIDS and passed away. In my church, this was a massive topic of debate. For many, God was using Rock Hudson to demonstrate to the godless that he was tired of having his commandments flouted. Because of Rock's status, God was proclaiming his sin from the rooftops and giving the rest of the gays a preview of coming attractions if they would not repent. It was ugly, mean, and vindictive, all done in God's name. Unfortunately, I was too afraid to discuss it from my perspective. So instead of letting them see how painful their judgment was, I nursed my wounds privately, nestled deep in my closet.

It was only a few weeks since my pastor dismissed Calvin's real pain and misrepresented God without even bothering to spend more than fifteen minutes with the kid, and I was still pissed about that. I continued to hang out with Calvin, but he was reluctant to talk about either of his experiences, the experience with my pastor or the experience in the church that his family was unfortunate enough to have visited.

During one particular Sunday service, our pastor wandered off on a tangent during his sermon. He was notorious for those departures into uncharted territories where he would spend vast amounts of time roaming the countryside trying to find a point somewhere deep in the quagmire he continued to get himself into. This day he wandered into the world of Christian rock—Ruh-Roh. This particular diatribe was about the ungodly behavior of the lead singer of the band, Whiteheart. Scott Douglas was convicted on three counts of aggravated sexual assault for having sex with minors, two girls. The pastor went off on an assault on all these sexual crimes (the gays included) and remarked that Scott couldn't have even been a Christian in the first place, or he would never have done such a thing.

Since I was a Christian and struggling so desperately with my sexual issues, I realized that this was a completely unfair assessment of how Christianity suddenly made us perfect in matters of sexuality. Being one of those people constantly on the other side of the Christian's judgment (though most of them never knew they were judging me—so they were judging me right to my face), I stood up and left the room and never returned. It was too much. I didn't mean to make a scene, but I did. Everyone watched me leave, though that was never my intention.

So, for the rest of my duration in Cody, I spent my Sundays attending the Bedside Baptist Church with Rabbi Sheets and Pastor Pillows.

I was getting frustrated with all things spiritual. I had always wanted a "music ministry," but I knew that would never happen as long as I was gay. I wanted to make my living as a singer/songwriter, but I couldn't change my orientation to make room for God's blessing.

This left me with another challenge to my spirituality. What was my motivation for changing my orientation? Was it God? Was it because I wanted to have music ministry so bad that I was willing to do anything to get it? I considered writing "secular" music, but I didn't feel like I had much to say in that realm. To me, sex and romance were nice, but there was something about God, about my desire for God, that I felt I wanted to communicate so I never fully considered a secular music career.

Whatever the real motivation, my life was on hold until I overcame this curse. Music was my love, and I was never happier than when I was writing and playing music. Still, I would never be able to express myself publicly until I was healed, and God didn't seem interested in facilitating that change.

This is where the God thing got weird for me. I felt helpless against my sexual orientation, and as a result, I felt hopeless about ever having that relationship with God I so deeply desired and that music career that called to me repeatedly. I blamed God because he held all the cards. He could heal me if he wanted to. Obviously, I was not going to be able to do this on my own, but God WOULD NOT help. My prayers were falling on deaf ears.

Why wouldn't he help me? He was the one who had the problem with it. If he had just left it alone, then I would be okay. And how could I be responsible for a "sin" over which I had no control? It was as if God had taken this "drive," put it inside of me, turned it up to 11, and then said... "Oh, by the way, you can't use it!"

Still, I focused on how much I needed and loved God and decided not to let it take me out of the game. I continued to pray and seek God, and my writing reflected that. I continued to go deeper, and my music became more authentic. It was my music that helped me make this journey. There were people around me who responded positively to my music. There was no question that I was connected with something, but when it came to the issue of my sexuality, God was unmoved.

After about a year in Cody, my mom was again transferred through her work. This time she was transferred to Billings, Montana. This was a welcome change for me because at least Billings had a population of over one-hundred thousand people. I was ready for the "Big City."

By now, we had moved from Riverton to Cody. We moved into a house that, from the outside, looked awesome, but during the winter, it was discovered that the house wasn't insulated. During a blizzard, we watched snow be driven through cracks in the boards. No matter how hard we tried, we could not heat the place. So we moved to another apartment on the corner where Yellowstone Ave—east to west, turned into Eight Street, headed north. Bringing the grand total of moves to 16. The move to Billings would put us at 17. We moved into a hotel for a few months until my mom could find a house, which she eventually did. A duplex on Terry Ave. So now we're at 18.

In Billings, I heard about a big church called the First Assembly of God. I was a little uneasy about it because it was too charismatic, but I tried it. It turned out that I liked it okay. The music was great, and I met some incredible people. One of my friends at First Assembly was an actor. He introduced me to a friend of his who was directing an improv group. When Elliot learned I was a writer, he invited me to the group. He thought that as a writer, I could help the group develop new scenarios and situations, which would help his actors improve their skills.

While there, Elliot had me participate in some of the exercises with the rest of the group. Well, it turned out that I wasn't bad at improv. The whole group liked me, and they asked me to join them. Needless to say, I did. We were pretty good at our craft, and before long, we performed live at bars, nightclubs, juvenile detention homes, and shopping malls. We had our theater that we both rehearsed at every Saturday morning and performed every other Saturday night.

Through this group, other acting opportunities started opening up for me. I was asked to play an extra in the college production of Jesus Christ Superstar. I was a Roman soldier. After the play closed, I went to the cast party. There was one cast member there who I thought was gorgeous. I had successfully ignored those feelings during the play when we had struck up a conversation or two. That night after the cast party, Zhan offered to give me a ride home. I took him up on it since it was late, I was tired, and it would be faster than walking. He asked if he could stop by his house first to pick something up, and I said fine. It was almost morning, and I was exhausted from partying all night.

On the way to the house, we played the questions game. Where are you from? What do you want to be when you grow up? What's your favorite Andrew Lloyd Webber musical? As we drove along, though, his questions got more personal. Then he said, as if he knew I may be getting uncomfortable, "Ask me anything you want to know about me."

We walked into his apartment and sat down, and continued talking. Again he asked me the same question. I didn't know what to ask, so I asked, " What do you want me to ask?" He looked at me carefully and asked, "Do you want to take a shower?" Of course, it was now daylight, I had been up all night, and I was starting to feel the effects of it, so I wasn't quite firing on all thrusters. I asked him, "Why do I stink?" That embarrassed him, and suddenly I realized what he was talking about.

I looked at Zhan's face. He was beautiful. All those feelings I had been trying to ignore were back. After a moment of silence, I told him yes, and we got into the shower. While I was with him, I was in ecstasy. We finished with the shower and went to bed. Lying next to him felt right to me. We lay in each other's arms for several minutes, and honestly, I didn't want to ever move again. With those thoughts in mind, I fell asleep and didn't wake up for several hours. When I did wake up, Zhan was still beside me.

We went out a few times, but I was overcome with guilt and fear that someone in my church would find out. I finally had to tell him what I was going through. He didn't understand, but that didn't matter. I had to do what I thought was right. So I ended the relationship, my second "relationship" to speak of.

Even though I did what I thought was right, I was angry, lonely, and frustrated. I was angry with God, so I rattled off my mantra, "Why won't He help me?" In a somewhat visible way, I lashed out. Some of my friends were worried, but there was no way I could tell them what was happening inside my head.

Only a few weeks previous, Calvin asked if he could come to Billings to stay with me. Of course, I agreed, and he came up. That's when he got to witness this rather severe meltdown. Like I said, this poor kid couldn't catch a break. Shortly after that, he decided to go back to Cody. It was just too intense for him.

Overwhelmed by all this emotion, I decided to take a considerable risk, and I went and talked to the church's associate pastor. I told him about my struggle and that I didn't know what to do. He recommended that I go to one of the therapists who attended the church and gave me his contact information. So I was now on my second therapist, my third counselor.

I spent about a year with this therapist, and in that time, I never felt we were making any progress, not even on some outlying issues. He prayed with me, had me talk about my feelings, anointed me with oil, cast [more] demons out of me, and took me outside to do some "guy" stuff like play ball. Still, nothing shifted. At his advice, I tried a technique that he called "aversion therapy." With this therapy, I would sniff a chemical whenever I thought about a man. It stank. It was the foulest odor I had ever smelled. He explained that my brain would replace the fantasy's pleasure with the odor's pain. I did this dutifully while I was his patient.

Our improv troupe was taking off, and we were experiencing a certain amount of local renown. After much deliberation, we finally chose a name for ourselves. We called ourselves *"Actors: and Other Diseases."* Stylistically we were similar to the popular TV show hosted by Drew Carrey, "Who's Line is it Anyway?" only we did this long before that particular show hit the airwaves.

I was again confronted with my sexuality because one of the guys in the group was gorgeous. My saving grace at the time was that he wasn't gay but could be flirty. This only enhanced my feelings toward him.

Even though I was a Christian, I must have looked like someone who desperately needed Jesus because people kept witnessing to me everywhere I went. I remember that after one particular show, the cast and some friends were eating at our favorite restaurant, and I was talking to a friend across the table. Some guy came up behind me and said, "I think you need this." I picked it up, glanced at it quickly, and set it back down on the table, never missing a beat in my conversation.

It was one of those "why you need Jesus" tracts. Everyone at the table was laughing at the way I handled the guy. They all thought it was me having fun with him. In reality, I thought it was a joke, and someone I knew was at the table.

Aside from the tension of working next to a gorgeous co-star, something else was happening to me. I found myself compromising with my spiritual ideals. Getting people to laugh is not always easy, and I have always had a blue sense of humor. Because of that, I found that I was often at odds with what I thought was right and what was not, but I stayed in the troupe until I left Billings.

After about a year in Billings, I was ready to move on to greener pastures. I had an aunt in Seattle, Washington. So I called and asked, 'If I could save up some money, could I stay with her for a while?' Knowing that it wasn't very likely that I would raise a lot of money in Billings, my aunt invited me to come out anyway and not to worry about the expense. So I moved to Seattle.

An interesting side note about Billings was that shortly after I moved to Seattle, I learned that the son of the associate pastor came out to his family and friends. I don't know how they all handled that, but I had met this boy. He was about my age, and there wasn't any doubt in my mind that he was gay. I just figured he was working on his own issues too. And a few years later, I would learn that he had taken his own life.

The move to Seattle would now put me at 19.

SEATTLE

The first few weeks in Seattle were some of the most difficult in my life. I didn't know anyone. I didn't have a job, spending money, a car, or a single friend. One Friday evening, my aunt dropped me off at a place called the *"Dance of Joy."* This was a place that played Christian dance music in an environment where Christians could hang out without the other trappings of nightlife. I sat in this place of about a hundred people and felt alone. Everyone around me was having fun, dancing, sipping their mocktails, laughing and sweating, and talking to one another. They all had friends.

To get to know people, I tried a couple of the larger churches in the area, but they were cold and unfriendly. The first church I attended, Overlake Christian Church, was so big that I knew it wasn't a place I would make friends unless I joined a smaller group within the church. Well, I liked music and singing, so I tried out for the choir. I freaked out, though, when I sat in the choir room, and they asked me to sign a contract stating that I would attend all rehearsals and performances. Not knowing the church, I had no idea how they would enforce the contract. Would they come after me legally if I missed a rehearsal? What would they do to me if I missed a performance? Was I signing an NDA and couldn't join another church or choir for so many years? This was disconcerting.

Another side note:

The lead pastor of Overlake, Bob Moorhead, and another man were arrested in a public restroom in Daytona Beach, Fla., for allegedly masturbating in front of undercover police officers. The case was later dropped, but allegations mounted against him, including seventeen members of his church who reported that he had sexually assaulted them. He eventually had to resign as the lead pastor. He was possibly another man losing the struggle to keep his beach ball underwater.

Going back to the dancehall: Outside the hall was a hill, and up on the hill was an area where several trees and bushes created a private clearing. I went up there where I could be alone and pray. While there, I had a raw conversation with God. A conversation in which I was honest about how I felt, and I didn't couch it in flowery or religious words. I talked with him candidly about my frustration, my loneliness, and the challenges I was facing then. Since my aunt had dropped me off, I couldn't just pick up and leave. I had to wait until the time we had decided that she would pick me up. So I was stuck, which made me angrier, and as I got angrier, I had more to say about it.

"Dammit, God!" I whisper-shouted into the air. "You know full well that I have not only been eager but that it's been my total desire to serve you with all my heart. So why can't you accept that? Either accept me or reject me but stop toying with me. Dammit!"

After the conversation, I went down and sat on the steps of the dance hall. I vowed that if anyone started talking to me about Jesus, I would let them have both barrels. For the moment, I was not a Christian (I knew that would change once I calmed down, but I was worked up), and I was ready to do battle against God if need be.

While I was sitting there, a guy came and sat beside me. He sat for a couple of minutes, then turned to me and held out his hand. "I'm Tom," he said. I was in shock. It had only been five minutes since my conversation with God, and already somebody was talking to me. I introduced myself and shook his hand.

Tom asked me the basic questions, where was I from, what did I do, and what church I attended? I told Tom that I was new to Seattle, didn't know many people, and was looking for a church. Tom told me about his church. I was interested, so Tom told me he had a friend who lived in my area and could pick me up that Sunday morning.

Tom's friend showed up on Sunday morning and took me to church.

Eastside Foursquare Church was also a large church in one of the Eastside Seattle suburbs. Eastside's basic philosophy was pretty simple. They wanted to create a healthy church with healthy members who could think for themselves. They trusted me with my relationship with God, and unlike any of the churches I had attended in the past, they didn't tell me how to think (or even how to vote, for that matter). And should I want to join any of their volunteer ministries, I would not be required to sign a contract.

On my first day there, the pastor told the congregation that God had instructed him to give away something valuable. He talked about how he argued with God for a while before finally giving in. He did it and still didn't feel great about it, but he was happy that he had been obedient. I immediately liked this guy, and this was a church that I could feel safe in.

Eastside Foursquare Church would be my home for the next fourteen years.

As time went on, I started meeting people. Many of them liked to sharpen their spiritual skills with one another through discussion, and it was rarely personal if we disagreed with each other. They were also far more open and honest with each other than I had seen in any other churches I attended. I felt safe there—except for that one thing.

Thanks to my involvement in the church and my new, extensive network of friends, I managed to "control" my thoughts (well, at least my actions) for about two years. I worked hard to keep that beach ball under the water without drawing attention to myself, but sure enough, it tried to surface again. When it did, it picked the worst possible time (don't they always?). Or, perchance, it was all the other circumstances that gave it the impetus to push up. I can't say.

I was gainfully employed and living in an apartment with a couple of guys I met at church. Aside from my aunt, the rest of my family was in Montana. My mom lived in Billings, and my sister had finally given up on her father and moved back in with our mom. My grandparents lived in Summers, and everyone else was in Kalispell, Whitefish, or Columbia Falls (what they call the Flathead Valley).

My grandfather (on my mom's side) was diabetic, and the disease was taking its toll on his body. I received a call one day at work from my sister informing me that my grandfather had had another heart attack and died. This hit me hard. It was his third in just as many years. During the other two, I was able to get to Kalispell and sit with him in the hospital. While I was there, we didn't talk much, but I would sit by his bed. My grandfather and I never talked all that much, but we were comfortable with silence. I think this was healing for both of us. There were so many times as I was sitting next to his bed chatting with him that I wondered if I shouldn't have offered at least some explanation as to why I went so crazy when I was a teenager, but I decided that it might not be good for his heart.

Perhaps it was because I was starting to recognize that we didn't have much time left, but I started reminiscing about our time together. As I did so, I discovered how much he had done for me. I recognized his sacrifices and all the time he stepped in to help. Now that he was gone, I could never tell him how much all that meant to me.

Before I left Seattle to head back to Montana for my grandfather's funeral, I was told that my job was ending and that my roommates were moving out. My roommates had a friend whose father owned a house, and they were all moving in together, and I was uninvited. All this coalesced to create what would become another pivotal point in my life and my relationship with God.

I was approaching the end of my endurance. I was anxious, and the struggle seemed to be out of control. Alone in my living room, frustrated and in tears, I told God I would not last much longer. This wasn't just a sexual thing; this was also a point where I was considering checking out for good. If I killed myself, then God would finally have to deal with me, and I was ready to take that extreme step. I was angry, and I wanted to force God's hand finally. Finally, we would stand face to face, and he couldn't hide behind his silence anymore.

So that night, I sat alone in the dark. I tried to find some music on the radio that might lift me up. While flipping through the channels with the remote, I passed the Christian radio station, and even though I rarely ever listened to it because the music was too mellow and cheesy, I decided I would leave it there. While listening, I heard an ad for an organization called Metanoia Ministries. They specialized in working with homosexuals who wanted to be free to live their lives for Christ.

Metanoia was part of an organization called Exodus International, and their whole purpose on the planet was to lead the homosexual out of his sins and into Biblical sexuality. They offered programs, counseling, classes, and other forms of reparative therapy to help get the Christian into the right relationship with Christ. So the following day, I was on the phone with Metanoia Ministries. They told me their location and asked me to come in for an interview.

> *Note: Ex-gay groups usually set up an interview because they're paranoid about being infiltrated by either a gay person looking to hook up or a gay advocate trying to convince their members that they cannot change.*

We talked at length about my struggle, and the counselor took me into the lobby and armed me with a plethora of literature to read. Therapy was based on a sliding scale (after all, if you're going to try to live the Biblical lifestyle, you'll have to pay for it). The problem, of course, was that this wasn't covered by insurance. Blue Cross didn't care that I was gay. Being recently unemployed made the finances of it even that much more complicated.

It was there that I was introduced to *Joseph Nicolosi, Elizabeth Moberly, Leanne Payne, NARTH, and the Family Research Institute*—a group that I call *The Cabal of Gay Torture*. I bought every book on the shelves and read every piece of information available to me. I worked hard in this group and never missed a session.

Okay, I did miss one.

I was living in Kirkland, one of the Seattle suburbs, and I was early for my appointment in downtown Seattle, so I found myself wandering around downtown (I didn't go downtown much because I was afraid that it would lead me into sin). While exploring the downtown area, I came across an adult bookstore and went in. This was the first time I had been in one of these, and as soon as I walked in, I could feel the blood rushing to my head (both of them). My breathing got tight, and I was almost numb from the fear, excitement, and lack of oxygen. I made a few purchases and immediately went home to enjoy my purchases. I called my counselor and told him my back had gone out. This was a believable excuse since I was in a close-call car accident in 1987, and to this day, I have severe back problems because of it. He believed me, and I rescheduled for next week. That appointment I did keep that and each one after that.

Along with the counseling sessions, they offered a class called *Living Waters*, and I signed up for that too. This class was intensive. We met once a week, and every night would start with a prayer, then we would sing some worship songs, then one of the leaders, a successful ex-gay counselor, would give us a talk. We would then break into small groups and do the work in the workbook. Then we would talk about our week and, if necessary, make our confessions. We were supposed to be held accountable to each other throughout the period of this program.

I spent several months in this class until it was finished, and then I joined a support group.

I was struck by several things in this group. The first was that nobody seemed to have a handle on their sexual orientation. Even the group leaders talked about how careful they had to be at all times. The devil was constantly tempting them, and if they weren't careful, they would find themselves off track. I also noticed that they kept changing the meaning of *"change."* Sometimes changing meant living a completely heterosexual life. At other times change meant altering your behavior and recognizing that you might always struggle with homosexual feelings. Occasionally, change meant that you would always "feel" gay, but if you couldn't get to the place where you could love a woman, you might have to choose to live a celibate life. It would be challenging, but God would help you through it. This last option was rarely used because there weren't many men willing to take that extreme step.

Many of the men in my group were married, and their marriages were suffering. Some days the wives would be supportive; other days, the wives would be threatening divorce. In truth, many of the men I attended these meetings with eventually divorced. More than just the marriages, though, were the family struggles. It wasn't just a man struggling with his homosexuality, then fighting with his wife, but kids were involved, and some of the families were so messed up that I didn't see any hope for them.

One friend, in particular, had two kids, both of them in Junior High. He met a guy, and he and this guy started going out. His wife knew about it, but she didn't divorce him. They stayed married, and eventually, my friend repented and returned to her. In the meantime, their kids were struggling in school, having problems with him, and they didn't know why.

Our Exodus meetings were as much about encouraging our friends to "hang in there" as they were about anything else.

Another thing I discovered was that everyone blamed their homosexuality for most—if not all—of their problems. They couldn't have a healthy relationship; it must be because they were gay. They had drug problems; it must be because they were gay. They had a drinking problem; it must be because they were gay. Our problems were tied to our homosexuality, and we were encouraged to do so. If I were to finally kick the gay habit, all of my other bad habits would soon follow. I would lose that extra ten pounds; I would suddenly start eating right; I would stop drinking; I would lose my drug addictions, my anger would subside, and I would have successful, happy, and stress-free relationships... if only I could conquer that pesky gay thing.

They also blamed pornography on being gay. The reason I felt compelled to masturbate was because I was gay. The reason I liked porn was because I was gay. Even worse, they considered that anyone who liked porn must have a sexual addiction. So the reason I walked into that adult bookstore that day was because I had a porn addiction, which had been latent until it finally had the chance to express itself.

My counselor told me that to be successful, I must stop masturbating altogether. When I was unsuccessful at this, it was because I had a sexual addiction. Every aspect of my sexuality was considered taboo, and until I surrendered it to Jesus and abstained from everything even remotely considered sexual, I would remain a slave to the addiction.

Note: In keeping score of how many times I've moved over the years, here are my Seattle moves: I moved from Billings to Seattle/Briar (my aunt's house). From my aunt's house to an apartment with my roommates in Kirkland (a suburb east of Seattle) To Beuna Vista Apartments (Kirkland) To a house in Redmond (also an Eastside suburb) to my friend John's house, to the Green House, to the "roommates" house in Kenmore, to the apartment on Bellevue Street on Capitol Hill in Seattle, to an apartment on Beacon Hill, to another apartment downtown Beacon Hill, to a house in South Seattle, to 7th and James Downtown Seattle, to Broadway, Downtown/Capitol Hill Seattle. The grand total here is 11 moves. 19+11=30

PORK LOINS

My first exposure to porn would have to be in the underwear section of the Sears catalog in the early 80s. That would remain my only source of titillation until I moved out to Seattle. For those too young to know, Sears would send out these giant catalogs advertising various products every so many months. And since they also sold clothes, there were many pictures of men and boys in underwear (women too, but I never paid attention to those).

I once stumbled across a Penthouse or a Hustler magazine that I found in a garbage can. I kept this hidden under my bed in my room. It had girls in it, but it also had guys. I was so excited. This was my first exposure to a naked man (remember, this is the eighties, and the internet didn't exist). Still, I never hung on to these things for fear that someone would find out about me.

In Seattle, while innocently searching the magazine rack for something containing crossword puzzles, I happened upon a couple of magazines like *Men's Fitness* and *Men's Health*. Later I would stumble upon a magazine called *International Male*. The bodies in these magazines were beautiful. I wouldn't subscribe to these magazines because I was afraid I would be giving in to my sinful urge, so I bought the magazine every month when it came out. I was starting a new workout regimen at the time, so nobody suspected anything (or they never voiced it anyway).

My first exposure to hard-core gay porn was that day in downtown Seattle, and I was determined not to let it get to me. So after a few weeks of owning the magazines, I burned them in my fireplace as a sacrifice unto the Lord and as a sign of my repentance.

Later that year, I met Sonya at church. Sonya was a beautiful blonde, and we liked each other. Because I liked her a lot, I thought that this time my relationship could be blessed by God. We started slowly, and she thought it was because of my Christian values, so she didn't initially suspect anything. We dated for a while until it became apparent that I couldn't be there physically. I could hug, kiss, and cuddle, but it was clumsy, and I couldn't get myself excited about the physical aspect of our relationship.

While Sonya and I were dating, I met Alex. I don't remember how we met, only that it was through church. Alex looked like Charlie Sheen. We all three hung out together, and I couldn't ignore that I wanted Alex more than I wanted Sonya. Sonya knew that something was wrong, and we began to fight. So to keep from hurting her, I came clean about what I was going through. Oddly enough, she understood and told me she would stick with me.

So now we were dating with full disclosure.

The problem with being open about something like this is that, like it or not, suspicion starts to set in. If ever I was late for our date, or if she didn't hear from me in a while, she invariably wondered what I was doing (this was before cell phones and texting). While she didn't always say anything, it was in her voice. Her biggest frustration with me was that I would often rather hang around with my guy friends than hang out with her.

We both realized that I couldn't be there for Sonya the way she needed me to be there, and we broke up. I was surprised at how depressed I was after the breakup. I wasn't sure if it was because I truly loved her or that I failed yet again. It was probably a little bit of both. The pinnacle of my healing was that I would finally be able to be intimate with a woman, and I still could not make that happen. I couldn't MAKE it happen no matter how I tried.

I failed. I failed God, I failed Sonya, and I failed me. Here I was, several years into this, and I was no closer to healing now than when I started.

TARPIT THEATER

It was an actor's dream—an actual paid gig as an actor. I couldn't believe how lucky I was. The gig was with a Christian theater company called TarPit Theater. At first, it seemed like a dream job. I would get paid to act and travel around the Northwest United States doing a job that made a difference in the world. We did three plays that dealt with substance abuse and family dysfunction, both near and dear to my heart. Each one of these plays was geared for different ages. One play was written specifically for grade school-age children, one for Jr. High School students, and the third for High School and College age students. This job was eye-opening on many levels.

I was surprised at how trusting most of the kids were when they talked to me about their own lives after the show. There's something about putting someone on stage that creates instant connection and instant trust. They trusted me because I was on the stage and portraying something so powerful and close to most of these kids' experiences. I usually played the heavy: the drug dealers and users and the troubled kid at home, which probably resonated with many. After almost every show, several young people would come up to talk and talk about how their lives seemed to mirror what they saw on stage. They couldn't talk about these things with their friends, and they especially couldn't tell their teachers, so they talked to me about it.

After listening to so many of these stories, I felt like I was on the front line of a major war and looking at so many casualties. I didn't know how to respond. I listened to other members of the group shell out advice, which was right out of the Bible (albeit couched in a modern language), but it did little to help these kids. I think it was here that I realized how much the so-called Christian ethic didn't and wouldn't work in real-life situations. Their whole focus was that drugs and sex were terrible, but there was no awareness of how deep these issues go. I knew why these kids were taking drugs. They were trying to feel better. They were trying to escape. I have never denied that while I was taking drugs, I felt good. That's why I did them, but all addictions begin and end in pain, and I was intimately aware of both.

So I started asking myself, "What could I say to these kids that would help them through some of these hideous events?"

TarPit was a small theater. It consisted of the founders, Matthew and his wife, and Trevor and his wife. Matthew and Trevor were the operations directors, and they decided which plays were produced and then cast and directed them. The only other person on staff was Flora, who handled the box office and other office administration affairs. During production, they would contract set designers and customers. They didn't pay any of their actors except the Road Company. That was me.

The Road Company was just that. The part of TarPit that took to the road. We traveled from town to town throughout the Northwest, performing for schools and church groups. On the road, we stayed with either a single host family who would put us all together or with more than one host who would separate us. There were five of us in the Road Company, three girls and two guys. Candice was the Road Company manager and occasionally acted as an actor when needed. It was her job to deal with all the administrative issues on the road (and while on the road, she was our boss). Then there were the four of us, two girls and two guys. We got along okay, but as with any group, we had challenges. The irony of this group was that the two guys were gay, and one of the girls was a lesbian. We didn't know it at first, but as time went on—things were revealed.

I never admitted what I was going through to anyone. I justified it by saying that I was afraid of the consequences, both at TarPit and in my church. The consequences would be bad at TarPit, but things would be okay at my church. I also used the excuse that I was "believing" in God's healing, so I refused to wear the label "gay." Instead, I pretended to be straight, telling myself I was *a new creature in Christ Jesus* and *"living as if..."*

Because it was most common to have two different host families when we traveled, it was guys in one place and girls in the other. Jeff and I spent much time together. During this time, we talked about many things. Jeff hinted that he was going through something significant that would get him thrown out of TarPit if they found out about it. When we talked, he would refer to this "issue" he was going through. As I listened to him, his words were intimately familiar. So one day, when we were alone, I asked Jeff, "Are you struggling with homosexuality?"

Jeff told me no that he wasn't "struggling" with it.

So I asked him, "Are you gay?"

He said yes, but that he wouldn't try to change. He couldn't. Of course, this was uncomfortable for me. I wasn't ready to hear that it was okay to be gay.

At TarPit, I was a lightning rod, and when I left, there were a lot of bad feelings. TarPit considered itself liberal, but in reality, they were only liberal compared to Ann Coulter or Rush Limbaugh. At Eastside, I had never thought too much about politics. I voted and was involved in political issues, but Eastside didn't espouse any political views, and they weren't very tolerant of people that pushed their views on others. They were there to find God, and everything else was that person's choice. So I never considered myself a liberal. As a matter of fact, in that particular election cycle, I voted for George Bush Senior against Dukakis.

When I took the job with TarPit, I became painfully aware that I was, in fact, liberal by their terms. I wasn't just politically liberal, I was also spiritually liberal, and I was chastised almost daily because of my "liberal" spiritual views. Sometimes, during our Bible Study/Touch In, I would weigh in with my spiritual views regarding whatever issue we were discussing.

I remember we were talking about the Book of Proverbs one day, and I mentioned that I didn't like Solomon. I felt that God had given him so much: money, wisdom, and influence, and yet he never used that wisdom for the good of Israel; in fact, he was horrible to his people. At that moment, Matthew, the owner, informed me that I had no right to feel that way because, in his words, "Solomon wrote the Bible." I pointed out that Solomon enslaved his people and indentured them so that he could build a temple to God. I also pointed out that when Solomon's son ascended to the throne, the Israelites begged him not to be like his father. When he refused, that's when Israel split into Judah and Israel.

Then there was the topic of money. Once I was talking about money, I mentioned that Jesus spoke more on the issue of money than he did on any other subject.

"Not according to my Bible," Marcy chided (Marcy was one of the members of the road company).

"Maybe you've just been reading the wrong Bible," I replied.

So that turned into a big fight. Strangely enough, the next day, an article turned up by a guy named Larry Burkett in which he pointed out that, in fact, "Jesus spoke more on the topic of money than on any other topic in the Bible." Still, I wasn't vindicated because they all looked away from me when they read it and never brought the subject up again.

I knew that Jeff and Janice (the other two actors) were more liberal, but they didn't talk about it. I guess they were bright and learned their lesson from me. We would sometimes joke about how liberal Marcy and Candice thought they were, but that was always between us.

TarPit represented Fundamentalist Christianity's true feelings toward many things, and the strongest was homosexuality. There wasn't a day that passed without some derisive comment toward homosexuals. This became harder and harder for me to take. After a while, I did what I usually do when I get upset. I said something.

A week previously, there had been a march for gay rights in Seattle. Trevor, the cofounder, was going on at length about the spiritual position this put our city in. He continued to "worry" that we were bringing our city closer to God's wrath.

The road company was having a workday, stuffing fliers, and sending out mailers, and I lost my head in frustration.

"I think God would be okay with giving his children basic human rights, even if they didn't see eye to eye with God."

Jeff and Janice looked at me. It looked like they were glad I said it, but the next thing I knew, I was soundly "rebuked in the Name of Jesus." Trevor quoted scripture and informed me that attitudes like mine only brought this city closer to God's wrath, and he chastised me for not taking my spirituality seriously. Then he went off on a tirade.

"This is the church's fault," he kept repeating. "We should never have allowed this to happen. We have abandoned God's command, and I take the blame."

Aside from being a drama queen, I felt that this man was trying to pretend he had "love," but he was confessing how much he abhorred these people. One knows love when one stands in the presence of love, and there wasn't even a shred of love in that place. Jeff and Janice, and I were just angry. Jeff thought I stood up because I was sensitive to his issue.

Later that year, a Family Values group decided to hold a Christian Family Values rally, and they chose Volunteer Park in Seattle as their location. There are hundreds of lovely parks in Seattle, but they chose to hold this rally in the only park in the city frequented almost exclusively by gays and lesbians; and gay-friendly people. Needless to say, there was a massive protest by gay rights activists.

This "event" was all I heard about for the next two months. Trevor, Matthew, and Candice went on and on regarding how they had been attacked simply because they represented Christian Family Values and that Satan himself was trying to destroy the family using these groups.

The fact that they could have held this rally at any other park didn't even cross their minds. The fact that they had done nothing but instigate problems with the gay community meant nothing. To them, all they saw was their righteous indignation. Even the right-wing talk radio stations in town were discussing the incident, and they all agreed on one thing: this gathering should have happened somewhere else. It appeared to all of them that the Christians wanted to start a fight.

A PRAYER AND A PIZZA

One night the Road Company did a show for a Seventh day-Adventist academy in a suburb south of Seattle. This academy was similar to Campion, where I had my disastrous freshman year. It was bizarre and frightening to be back at an Adventist academy so close to the one I attended in Colorado.

We arrived on campus early in the afternoon, ahead of our show that evening, so I had several hours to reflect on my experience at Campion. The more I thought about it, the more troubled I was. Tony's comment, "Faggot"; being kicked out; trying to hide my beach ball; all those memories came rushing back. I was miserable, and the others thought I was just being melodramatic. So I went into a corner to pout and try to console myself (and yes, wallow in some melodrama).

During the show, I had a panic attack in the middle of one of my scenes and nearly couldn't finish. I was afraid I would have to leave the stage. This wasn't the first time I had ever had a panic attack, but this was one of the worst (and most inconvenient). At this point, though, I did not know what a panic attack was. We hadn't discussed those in therapy. I suddenly went numb throughout my body, and I got a strange sensation that I was going to pass out on stage or forget my lines and that I was going to freak out in front of all these people and act crazy. My chest tightened, and I could hardly breathe. My heart was pounding so hard I thought I might be having a heart attack. I wanted to run off stage and hide before things got out of control.

I didn't do any of those things, however. I sat on the stool I had been sitting on, focused all my energy on Janice's face, and ran my lines mechanically until I could calm down. I was scared to death, and it turns out I scared everyone else too. They could all see on my face that something was wrong. They could see the terror in my eyes, and now they were worried; what would happen if I couldn't go on? How would they handle it if it happened? After the show, they asked me how I was doing, and I had a brief chance to tell them of my previous experiences with a Seventh-day Adventist school, carefully omitting the story of Tony and his remark, of course. After the show, many students and faculty came up and talked to us. They were kind and generous, and I was in a much better place than I had been in Campion. All in all, there was healing in that event, regardless of how terrifying it was.

A few weeks later, I was channel surfing and stopped on one of those television evangelists talking about the differences between demon oppression and demon possession. My ears perked up, considering my recent attack on stage. So I listened. He explained that Satan could not actively possess a Christian but could oppress them. Usually, I would have been skeptical, but I was more than willing to entertain the idea in light of my own attack (and since I didn't know what it was).

Eastside Foursquare Church had a large singles group at the time, and they met every Friday night. I looked forward to those Friday nights when I was in town and could attend the services. Our singles pastor was also the associate pastor, and he was a man I considered to be trustworthy and respectable. He was also funny and a darn good speaker.

I had been involved at Eastside almost since I started attending the church, and I had been there for several years, so Kyle Martin knew who I was. After the Friday night service, I approached him. I planned to ask him my question and see what his response was. I asked him if he believed that the Devil could oppress Christians.

"The short answer is 'Yes,'" he said. Then he briefly explained the difference.

That was all I needed to know. I could set my skepticism aside. That explained my experience on stage. I was satisfied with his answer, but he asked me to stick around for a minute. He quickly finished his conversations with those around him and took me into another room behind the stage, and we talked. He wanted to know what was happening, so I told him about my bizarre experience on the stage during my performance.

After the lengthy explanation, we concluded it was just a panic attack. He explained what they were, and I was completely okay with that. I preferred panic to demon oppression. It also made sense since my first experience with an Adventist academy was traumatic. So I got up to leave, but he insisted we pray together before I go.

While he was praying for me, he looked up at me and said, "I don't know if this is God or the pizza, you decide, But I feel like God is saying to you, 'You're not gay.'"

I freaked out. Now the pastor knew, the pastor of an extremely large church. Now there was the potential for everyone in my church to find out. My ability to stay involved in the church was threatened; my job at TarPit was threatened, but more importantly, my protective layers of secrecy were threatened. I was now vulnerable on an epic scale. Despite my attempts to hide it, all I could do was cry. I had been struggling with this issue for so long that once it was out in the open, it was like tearing the scab off an infected cut and letting all the puss drain out. I realize this is graphic, but that is, realistically, just how it felt.

When it first happened, I was frustrated with God. How could he reveal my personal information to someone else, especially someone as potentially risky as Kyle Martin? But as I thought of this, something occurred to me. Maybe God told Kyle because he knew that I needed to work through some of these feelings and because he knew that he (actually, both God and I) could trust Kyle.

After a few hours, I felt my spirits lifting. Release had to be just around the corner. All those years, all that pain, all those memories, they were all about to culminate in the final wrap-up where I was, at last, a heterosexual man who could love women, physically and emotionally. In my excitement, I stopped by a video store on the way home, and I rented a gay porn video.

I don't know why I rented the video. I think much of it had to do with the problems with TarPit. I was preparing for a month-long tour with them, and I couldn't bear the thought of being in that environment for that long. That weekend I bought a case of beer, and I proceeded to get as drunk as I possibly could. I was fully aware of the irony of what I was doing; a guy who talked about and focused on alcohol abuse with thousands of students was now so drunk that he could barely walk.

MICKEY AND THE EX-GAY GROUPS

When the school year finally ended, my contract with TarPit was over. I was never so glad to be away from any place. Emotionally I was a complete mess. I knew that deep down in my heart, I loved God and wanted to serve him completely, but TarPit had made me feel like I was nothing but a rebellious reprobate and that I was deceived into believing I was anything close to being a good Christian. They challenged me; they challenged my integrity; they challenged my spirituality—the complete opposite of how Eastside treated me.

It took me several years to deal with these feelings and finally come to a place where I could say the name TarPit without being drawn back to that place of pain, anger, and frustration. I know what you're going to ask because everyone does. So let me tell you now—I have forgiven them. I still talk about them as I do because they still stand as a defining moment in my life when I saw Fundamentalism's true colors. They represent Evangelicals' attitudes toward those who don't fit into their narrow view of "morality," they represent the lengths Fundamentalists will go to push their agenda, regardless of how many people they hurt along the way.

Because of my exposure to these arguments, I started to see behind the scenes. Everyone who disagreed with the Fundamentalist was considered hateful. I knew one guy who repeated over and over, "They hate me because I'm a Christian." I finally told him, "No, they hate you because you're an asshole." I am convinced that regardless of personal and political differences if these people acted like the Jesus presented in the gospels, they would be loved, respected, and listened to.

The pundits continue to talk about this thing called the homosexual agenda. They think that our whole purpose is to turn the world gay. They're so afraid of that because that's precisely what they intend to do—convert the whole world. Any Christian, who isn't actively out proselytizing, is not following the command of Matthew 28:19 to *"Go make disciples of all men."* They go door-to-door, stand on the street corners with bullhorns, hand out fliers, pamphlets, and tracts, and crash Pride parades, all attempting to win over just one more convert.

They don't understand that even if we wanted to, we could not convert one Soul. I had a major crush on my best friend, who was straight. We could talk about it, joke about it, and he was intrigued by it, but it could never go further. You don't just put on sexuality; it's who you are at the heart of who you are. Our so-called agenda frightens them because they know what their agenda is, and they're afraid we will interfere. If people open up to the fact that gays and lesbians are also children of God, they're less likely to take the Fundamentalist's side when they come calling.

Another thing I took away from this experience was that the Christian pat answers didn't work. These kids were suffering, and I hadn't been prepared for their brand of pain. It seemed to me that to tell them to put their suffering in the hands of God was diminishing their genuine struggle. Some of these kids lived in "Christian" homes, so Jesus obviously wasn't the answer here. As with my struggle with homosexuality, God didn't seem interested in helping these kids. I realized that if I was going to help these kids, I had better open myself up to the "wisdom" of God, whatever that happened to look like.

Believe it or not, that approach also got me in trouble. Even if I joked with them on their level, I was chastised.

One day in particular, we were at a high school, and we were invited to have lunch with the teachers. So we were all sitting around talking. Most of the teachers I met loved talking about their students, and these teachers were passionate about their jobs. They, too, were opening up to what they saw in their students' lives and looking for ways to help that wouldn't get them in trouble with the law or the school board. One of the teachers announced that she would come back as a therapist in her next life to help.

I joked that I would come back as a telephone so that I would have someone to talk to. It was a decent joke, and it got a laugh. Candice immediately said she was looking forward to going to Heaven.

I didn't think much about it, but after lunch, when we were alone, she chastised me for the joke. Her problem with it was that I should know better. There was no such thing as reincarnation, and I should be promoting the gospel of Christ.

Well, I had enough at that point. I shot back that it was a joke. It was a joke. A joke. A joke. Secondly, I told her, as far as I knew, I had never died before, so there was no way I could say with authority that we didn't come back.

Ultimately, if I was going to be any good to the people I was coming in contact with, I had to do it on their level and not expect them to come around to my point of view. In truth, I had nothing to say that would help them. However, I was surprised to learn that when these people felt listened to from a safe place, they often came up with their own answers. All they needed from me was my support and my genuine concern.

Kyle Martin's words continued to haunt me. Around every corner, I looked for my breakthrough to come. Around every corner, I looked for God's power to break into my frailty and deliver me. My relationship with God was doing well. I never let go of the hope that I would emerge from this struggle stronger and closer to him than I had ever been. Still, to help me facilitate this emergence, I elicited the help of more therapists.

One therapist kept calling everything I told her "my fantasy" about life. When she would talk to me, she would say, "In your fantasy of life..." this would happen, or "In your fantasy of life..." This is true. I was so annoyed with her. She was calling my struggle a "fantasy." I finally gave up and left her. I was paying her good money to dismiss all my feelings as fantasy.

At one particular service, Harvey Johnson, the head pastor of Eastside church, spoke on the ways in which God spoke (and still speaks) to his people. He pointed out that the best way to tell if someone was speaking for God was to wait and see if their words came true.

It had been a couple of years since my original conversation with Kyle Martin, so I decided to talk to Harvey. This was frightening to me because that meant I had to tell the head pastor of my church my sinister secret. But I needed to reconcile what Kyle had said with my persistent struggle, and I needed to understand why healing wasn't forthcoming, especially since someone with the spiritual integrity of Kyle predicted it. I explained to him what Kyle had said to me and that I was still not seeing any evidence that things were turning around.

Harvey listened attentively, and then he introduced me to Mickey. Mickey was a member of Eastside who "used to be gay" but now had overcome his sexuality and was successfully living his life as a heterosexual man. In fact, he was married, had two teenage boys, and was now leading a group of his own into heterosexuality.

I met Mickey at a local Starbucks, and we had a long talk. I told him about what I was going through, and he listened. After our conversation, Mickey told me about his journey. He had made it. He was where I wanted to be. Mickey also ran an Exodus group: A group of men and women in all stages of finding their way out of the Deathstyle (a term they use instead of lifestyle). So I went to my first Mickey Meeting. In front of all those guys, I tried to talk about how much I wanted to be free to serve God and only ended up falling to pieces and embarrassing myself, but they seemed accepting, nonetheless.

I was part of Mickey's group for several years, and I enjoyed it. I felt better now that I had a support group that I could talk to. Life was good. Okay, I almost drove my car off the road a couple of times while staring at a guy's ass that just would not quit, but I kept telling myself that would change. As Mickey put it, we were "healing heterosexuals."

I spoke with two therapists at that time. One therapist, Reuben, and I had some candid talks about homosexuality. Reuben told me, carefully and delicately, that he wasn't sure that there was anything that could be done to change anyone's sexual orientation and that instead of trying, I might be better off approaching my Christianity as a homosexual, and that I could apply all the rules about fidelity and morality within the confines of a homosexual relationship.

I liked Reuben a lot, but I wasn't yet ready to hear that. I still believed that God wanted me to be straight, and I was determined that I was going to make it.

I found another therapist who also attended Eastside. He specialized in helping men who were trying to overcome their homosexuality. I talked with him for as long as my insurance would pay for it, which was about six months.

Like most therapists before him, the first thing he tried to do was determine where and when I was molested and by whom. Ex-gay therapy relies heavily on the notion that molestation is the most common occurrence in a child's life to turn him gay. When I couldn't think of anyone who had molested me, then it was who I was trying to cannibalize. Another belief the cabal teaches is that cannibals only eat people with the skills and characteristics they want. If they want to be a good hunter, they eat the hunter. If they want to be fast, they eat runners. Therefore, another reason we were gay was that we were trying to make that masculinity a part of ourselves.

Having no success with any of those red herrings, we returned to my father. It had to be my father. During that process, he told me that I needed to write a letter to my father, calling him to account for his actions. I didn't want to have any communication with my dad, but the therapist knew best, and he assured me that this was the best way for me to grow as a man. He told me about many of his other clients who had done the same thing and found themselves set free from their homosexual past. So I took his word for it, and I wrote the letter.

I told my father exactly how I felt about how he treated me as a child. I told him honestly how I felt that he had abandoned me and that I wondered why, after all these years, he hadn't made a single effort even to contact me. I let my therapist read it to ensure I had included everything.

Oddly enough, my father wrote back. He was not happy with the letter, and he let me know that in no uncertain terms. He told me that my letter gave him the idea that I wanted an apology and that's the one thing I would never get from him. Needless to say, I didn't feel anything like my therapist said I would. So I wrote back one more time and told him that while it may be true that I would never get that apology, a real man would be more than willing to acknowledge the wrong and harm he had caused another person, especially if that person was his own son. I told him that a real man would walk on his knees to make peace with the son he had so violently injured. But I accepted that as he was not capable of behaving like a real man.

That letter made me feel better, but it still did not have the effect my therapist said it would.

Then my insurance ran out, and there wasn't any way I could pay the overwhelming amount of money that my therapist wanted for our therapy sessions. So when we talked on our last day, his final words were, "Well, when you get the money, I'm here."

I was so angry to hear that. This wasn't just a little problem. To me, it was spiritual life or death. I was trying to find a way to give my life totally to God, and all he cared about was the money—and he was a Christian. He knew my eternal salvation rested on this.

I left there feeling more discouraged than ever in my struggle so far. "What am I supposed to do?" I asked God. Again, there was no answer.

TINA

I returned to the Dance of Joy, but this time as a DJ. They had regrouped and changed their name to Radical for Jesus (RFJ). They held several events, including bonfires, retreats, and, of course, the dance. It was through this group that I met Tina.

We were at a retreat sponsored by the group on a lake just below Mt Rainier. Tina was a fiery redhead with the most fantastic personality of any woman I had met up to that point. She was beautiful, intelligent, compassionate, and sincere and wanted nothing more in her life than to give it entirely over to God. We were kindred spirits. What was more, she liked me. We liked spending time together. We went on walks, talked to each other for hours, and sometimes sat silently, staring at the beauty of the campsite around us. I remember we were sitting on a dock over a lake one night. It was late and very dark. We talked some, but we mostly stared into the sky and soaked in the starry beauty. As we sat, a shooting star so large it lit up most of the sky shot past us; its reflection shone in the water, acting as a mirror, making it look like two shooting stars were approaching each other. We watched this for nearly a minute until it finally burned itself out. It was so beautiful and amazing that we could barely breathe. I whispered into the night, "Do it again, Daddy." It was so wonderful. Maybe it was even a sign? Of all the girls I had ever met, Tina was the closest I had ever come to being in love. I believed it was possible that Tina could be the one girl who would break my curse.

As we spent more time together, I was convinced this was it. Tina was God's answer to me. I was finally going to be free.

Then came the same seemingly unalterable problem: I couldn't get physically intimate with her. I loved her mind and spirit, and quite frankly, her body was incredible too, but not to me. I loved her body the way most gay men love women's bodies. It was art. It was Van Gough, but I was looking for a Man Gough. Her body was something

I would rather admire with my eyes, not with my hands. We got close emotionally but not physically, and as I started experiencing the same frustration, I couldn't bring myself to go through it again. So I never told Tina anything, and I kept it as friends. I never officially asked her to go out with me. Tina believed it was the man's duty to initiate the date, and that let me off the hook. We could go to various places together, but I didn't have to commit to a "date officially." Then when she announced that she was dating a friend, I felt betrayed, angry, and hopeless again. Again I felt like I was a failure. I said nothing. I was angry at her, angry at my friend, and angry at the situation. Fortunately, my love for Tina made it possible for me to work through some of that, and eventually, I could ask God to bless their relationship.

BRAD

I began attending Eastside Foursquare Church in the summer of 1987, and it was now 1998, and I was still firmly ensconced in my role at the church. I was not only attending the church but also intensely active there. I sang backup vocals, wrote comedy sketches, directed the plays and drama, and helped with the singles group. That's where I met Brad.

Brad was the son of one of the associate pastors at Eastside Church. At first, the only thing we had in common was that we were both musicians; more to the point, we loved to write music, specifically electronic music. As we hung out together, our friendship grew. Brad was also open about his sexuality. He was straight, but he didn't mind talking about sex. This started to open up doors inside of me that I had never let open. I had never talked about sex as if it was a good thing. Brad did, and he wasn't embarrassed about that.

Brad was bothered by the fact that I didn't say too much about women. He couldn't figure out why. I continued denying him that I was gay, but in his mind, if I wasn't chasing women, then I must be gay. One night we were drinking and having fun. We both had a lot to drink and then Brad told me he felt sexual tension between us. At first, I didn't feel it, but when he said that, I realized there was something there, and I freaked out. We went for a walk outside and talked about it; it was finally out in the open.

The next few months were difficult for me because this was the first crush I had ever had where the person I had the crush on knew how I felt, and he didn't take off running like anyone else would have. I guess we needed each other for whatever reason.

Another issue that Brad hammered on was whether or not God meant for me to be straight. He wasn't sure that I should be trying to change my orientation. He wondered if we didn't just misunderstand the issues around sexuality, and maybe God created us as sexual beings and meant for us to behave as sexual beings. That was difficult for me to hear. I had invested most of my life trying to turn myself around, and every time he suggested that I didn't need to try anymore, I felt a sense of despair well up inside me. Still, I couldn't get that nagging thought out of my head that he might be right, and if he was, then what would I do? Where would I turn? What would Mickey say? Would I ever get those years back that I had wasted?

My relationship with Brad was complicated. I had always been proud that I was independent and would never let anyone control me or make demands on me. This worked for all the women I "dated," but it didn't work for Brad. Suddenly I wasn't so independent.

OUTED LIKE IT'S 1999

The year was 1999, and we were rapidly careening toward the end of the century, the end of the millennium, and the end of the world as we awaited the destructive Y2K bug to destroy our civilization.

By now, I had been contracting with the Microsoft Corporation. My job involved researching Internet search engines (this was pre-Google). I tested how accurate various search engines were when asked fully formed questions. As a result, I was exposed to many things I had never been exposed to before. While completely innocuous, some of the searches we did in these tests returned some dicey pages. One such question we entered asked for information about grizzly bears. That's when I learned that a bear was a big, hairy homosexual. Silly me, I had always thought it was a big, furry, four-legged mammal that liked to eat fish and berries and hibernate in the winter.

While working at Microsoft, I lived in a house with two Born-Agains. I had been there for about a year. Gene owned the house, and Larry and I were tenants. I volunteered at my church extensively, writing sketches for the services, directing the Christmas plays, and singing backup vocals.

Another of my other extracurricular activities was traveling with Mickey and his group to churches around the Puget Sound area. Mickey was "educating" the church on the issues surrounding homosexuality. His goal was quite commendable. He was trying to help the church understand homosexuality and to dissuade some of the passionate and angry emotions around the issue so that gay people in the churches today didn't have to go through what so many of us had gone through in our churches. So I wrote sketches for him and even performed in some of them. I was loving life. God was allowing me, finally, to live out my dream. Writing, performing, and traveling were my true passions. Unlike TarPit, I was accepted and supported as a

Christian, and those around me considered me a conduit of wisdom, not a messenger from Satan or some Liberal reprobate.

Despite all this success, I was still attracted to men, and that attraction was getting stronger than it had up to now. My beach ball was inflating and wanted to surface. The only way to describe these intense feelings to you would be to say, "Starve yourself for a week or two, and then stand in front of the buffet table at your favorite restaurant." That was the power of these emotions, and it was getting harder and harder to suppress them.

One day during lunch at Microsoft, I decided to go up on the Internet and research gay bars in Seattle. (I should point out that this was not illegal, as I wasn't surfing for porn, I was merely looking for an established business.) At the time of my search, only a couple of them were online, so I checked them out to see what they were like. At one bar, I met a guy who introduced me to the bathhouses in Seattle. At the bathhouse, I could have sex with anyone who wanted to. It was easy. You walked around in a towel. Then other guys would pass you, and if they were interested, they would give you a look—or even a touch. If you looked back or responded, then you were hooked up.

This was my first time with a man in a long time, and it was amazing. During the whole time I was there, I was in ecstasy. I used the opportunities to experience all those things I had thought about in my fantasies but had never tried. I ran my hands up and down his body, experienced the physical connection with him, and felt free.

I left the bathhouse and went home. I felt free for the first time in my life. However, that freedom soon changed to guilt. The next day, I felt so guilty that I went over to Mickey's house and, through many tears, told him what had happened. Then I cried and "repented," and we prayed together.

I still wrote sketches for Eastside and sometimes performed in them, though I felt somewhat hypocritical. For the next few months I stayed "straight" and avoided downtown Seattle at all costs, but I couldn't get the memory of those men out of my head. So, I went out one Friday night to a bar to hang out and see what it was like. I was new to the scene, so I didn't do much but observe. There was something powerful about watching these men show affection toward each other and do so publicly and without shame. It was something I had never seen except in the videos I rented, which wasn't affection; it was just bad acting. Watching this happen in front of me was amazing.

They were free, and open. They didn't have to hide from anyone. Their beach balls were on top, riding the water. I don't know what happened to me that night, but I couldn't get it out of my head how nice it must feel to just be myself. I think my beach ball had finally gotten the better of me, and despite all of my efforts otherwise, it had surfaced.

Before long, I signed up for an internet dating service and met a few people. I even joined a baseball team for the gay league. It was like having a new family, and I loved life. All my Christian friends were impressed that I was doing something that involved sports. Even Tina couldn't stop saying how proud she was of me. But I never told them which league I was in.

The new millennium was now upon us, and while everyone around me worried about the Y2K bug, I worried about where my life would go from here. Now that I was experimenting, what did that mean? Would I keep trying to change, or would I give up? I was indeed on the verge of a significant decision that I wasn't sure how I was going to be able to make.

One Friday night, I went to my favorite bar and drank too much. I didn't want to drive home in that condition, so I spent a few hours at the bathhouse. Of course, when I tell my friends that this was why I was at the bathhouse, they all look at me and nod in a sort of "if that's what you want me to believe, that's what I'll pretend we believe" sort of way. The bathhouse was attractive because I had just come out and didn't know anyone. This was a way to experience that connection or experience I had been longing for most of my life.

The next night, Saturday night, my sister Rachel, who was now a flight attendant for American Airlines, living in Boston, came into town. So I went to visit her along with several of my friends from church. We all had a fun time and stayed up late and reminisced. We separated when the restaurant closed. I got up early on Sunday because I had a ball game in the morning. Sunday afternoon, the teams were invited to one of the local bars. At the bar, I met somebody who wanted to take me home with him. We had a great time, and I spent the night at his place. The following day, on Monday, I went home before work to shower and change my clothes.

When I got home, I found a note on my pillow from my roommate, which read, "Benj, the police were here asking some serious questions… What's going on, Ben?" Attached to the note was a card from a police officer, and below that was his title and division. "Detective: Homicide." Immediately, I was concerned because I thought that someone I had met on Friday night must have been killed, or worse, something happened to one of my friends. So I picked up the phone and called the number on the card.

The first thing the detective said to me was that he wanted to know what was going on at the club over the weekend and why I didn't stick around when my partner went into convulsions. I was confused because I never saw anyone go into convulsions. I told the officer that, and he got a little irritated.

"You're not in any trouble," he kept reiterating, "I just want to know what happened."

"I don't even know what you're talking about," I told the detective.

"Look, the guy died, and we want to know why."

"If someone had died next to me, I think I would have remembered it."

"We have proof that you were there."

"I'm not denying I was there, but nobody died when I was there, at least not that I was aware of."

"You're not in trouble; we just need the truth."

"And I'm telling you the truth."

The argument went like this for over a half-hour. Finally, he said, "Look, we have it on video surveillance tape."

So I said, "I'm going to shower and get dressed, and then I'm coming down to the station, and we can look at this tape." I asked for his address and told him it would take me about a half-hour to an hour to get showered and downtown.

At that point, he backed down a little and started taking a less accusatory tone.

Eventually, I was able to ascertain that this guy they were talking about died on Saturday night, the night I was with my sister and our friends, not on Friday night, the night I was actually at the club. But the damage was done. The police had visited the Born-Agains, and I was officially "outed." That massive decision I was on the brink of making had just been made for me.

Needless to say, this was a strange and challenging time for me. I first had to sit down with my roommate, who owned the house, and talk with him. Gene told me he was pretty surprised and didn't know what to do. He was also a friend of Tina's (he met her through me), and because he was so freaked out, he went to her house and asked her if she knew anything about my lifestyle. She didn't, and she was as surprised as he was, but that explained a lot that happened between us.

Tina and I hadn't talked in a while, but I suddenly got a message on my voicemail from her asking how I was doing. I knew then that Gene must have talked to her, but I also knew Tina and that she was concerned about me. She knew I was about to embark on a difficult journey and wanted to be there for me. That meant more to me than anything that had happened between us up to that point.

As a result of the police visit, the Born-Agains didn't want me living with them anymore. They were just too freaked out. They couldn't handle it even if I planned on "repenting" and going straight. So I would be looking for a new place to live. My contract with the Microsoft Corporation was up that month as well, and so I would be looking for another job and another place to live, both at the same time. On top of that, I had to leave my church. Word was trickling out about my precarious situation, and they weren't about to let me continue writing or performing for them. Ultimately, though, I couldn't handle all the whispering. Remember, this was a big church, and I was pretty visible there (and had been for years), so I disappeared.

Most of the people stopped talking to me altogether.

All this happened around Mother's Day, 2000. This meant I had to take my mother to dinner and tell her why I was coming out after all this time, even though coming out was never my plan. After spending fifteen years trying to drown my beach ball, that ball was floating conspicuously along the surface.

Thanks to the police, I was coming out in a way that would not allow me to return to the closet even if I wanted to.

We went to my mom's favorite restaurant. We talked briefly about what had just happened; then, she told me that she wanted to talk about it in a more private place so that she could cry. That was the last thing I needed to hear. I told her that if she needed to cry, then I couldn't talk. It was simply too much for me.

She had brought her little New Testament and wanted to read a couple of scriptures to me.

"Do you think I haven't researched this?" I asked her.

Her response was, "Humor me."

So I listened to her read her scriptures, one out of Romans and the other out of Corinthians. She got to Corinthians, where Paul said, *"Neither the sexually immoral nor idolaters nor adulterers nor male prostitutes nor homosexual offenders..."* I pointed out another part of the scripture further down, which she hadn't noticed, *"And that is what some of you were."*

After reading that, she couldn't understand why I wouldn't keep trying.

I was through trying. Fifteen years were enough, and now that my proclivities had been "proclaimed upon the rooftops," I may as well take advantage of the newfound freedom that had been foisted upon me.

Soon after that, I talked to my sister on the phone. She already knew, but it was a matter of time before I told anyone.

The next few weeks were tumultuous ones. I got a letter from Mickey in an e-mail officially asking me to leave Exodus, but he was sure to include a statement saying that as soon as I wanted to get things right with Jesus, I would be welcome there again.

Through a strange coincidence, I was at my new favorite bar and ran into a guy I used to work with at Microsoft. We were in the same group but in different offices, so we never really talked to each other but knew each other.

When he saw me at the bar, he was surprised. He had no idea. I told him about what had recently transpired, and he just happened to be looking for a roommate in the Capitol Hill area of Seattle (that's where all the bars and the greater gay community are located). This was perfect for me because it put me where the action was. I was now within staggering distance from the clubs. The next few weeks were spent moving, job hunting, moving out of my office at Microsoft, getting resettled in my new apartment, and job hunting some more, wondering if anyone from my church was going to call me at least and see how I was, job hunting, wondering if anyone from Exodus was going to call and check in on me, job hunting, and job hunting some more.

Amidst all this, I called my friend Corey and asked if we could get together for lunch. Corey is one of those friends I have cherished for a long time. He was one of the first people I met when I started attending

Eastside, and we became close friends as soon as we met. Corey and I got together and chatted. The first thing that Corey said to me was that although he didn't understand, he knew me and knew that I had given this decision much thought. It was a quiet, off-the-cuff statement, but it meant more to me than anything anyone else had said. He was the first person to say that he knew me and trusted that I had given this decision the attention it deserved.

He was right. I had been thinking about this decision for months (even years) before I made it (or before it was made for me). While it seemed as if it just happened suddenly, it took years to get me to the point where I could have been able to make the decisions I made and live with the consequences that followed.

There's so much more to this story that I don't know if I could tell it without bogging it down, but these events all brought me here to this point, where I could walk out of "my closet," let my beach ball surface, and be who I truly was without feeling guilty and without fear.

SEPTEMBER 11, 2001

My sister Rachel became a flight attendant with American Airlines in the early nineties and was transferred to Boston for her first gig. She was there until she was transferred to Dallas/Fort Worth in 2000—where she lived when I came out. We talked often on the phone but could never talk face-to-face, which would have made the transition much easier for her. My transition was tough on her, too. I think a lot of it had to do with our Christian (and often Fundamentalist) upbringing.

It was in Boston that she met her friend, Jeff. Even after she left Boston, she and Jeff stayed close. Since they were both flight attendants, they were mobile, and it was easy for them to see each other often, even though they lived a thousand miles apart.

When I came out, it was in Jeff that she found comfort. Jeff wasn't her brother; he was an unbiased observer. He was also gay and had his own coming-out stories to tell. He could walk with her through our transitions and took great pains to help her understand where I was coming from. I met Jeff once when I visited Rachel in Boston, but I was still hiding in my closet then, so I pretended I was straight, and we didn't talk too much.

In February 2001, I was shopping at a local mall on Capitol Hill. As I walked toward the bathroom, a beautiful man walked past me. He was gorgeous... and what a body. I was shy, and I didn't say anything to him. We looked at each other as we walked through the mall, but that's about as far as it got. I figured it was fun flirting.

About two nights later, I went to a video store in that same shopping center, and he was there looking at videos with his friend. So I watched him out of the corner of my eye, but still, I never said anything. I found a video shortly after he found a video, and I ended up in the line right behind him. As I was standing in line, he and his friend were talking about business cards. He told his friend, "Everybody has business cards," and to prove it, he turned around and asked me if I had a business card. Well, I did, and I gave it to him, whether he was serious that he wanted it or not.

Sterling called me the next day, and we talked. We set our first date for March 1st, as we were only a few days away from the end of February. The next day after our phone conversation, Seattle experienced a big earthquake, measuring 6.4. We both took it as a sign. We were about to shake things up.

In March of that year, my roommate announced that he was moving in with his boyfriend, so I spent the next two months trying to find a new roommate. By May, I had had no success and couldn't afford to live in that apartment alone. Sterling and I were only dating, but he also needed a roommate because his roommate was moving about the same time. We discussed moving in together. It was soon, we both knew that, but it seemed there weren't many options. Again, the Universe was giving us a sign.

As a side note, I've said this many times but still find it fascinating. I don't consider myself a drama queen, but my life's weird events and coincidences are so dramatically compelling.

I resisted moving in with Sterling because we didn't know each other well and were getting into this relationship. However, since I could not find another roommate, and he couldn't either, I took it as a sign from God that this was my next step, and I moved in with him.

Early in the morning in September, I was wakened early in the a.m. by my sister, Rachel. She told me to turn on my T.V. and watch. I'm so glad she called since she was an American Airlines employee. I turned on the T.V. just in time to see the second plane hit the second World Trade Center. Shortly after that, they broke with the story of a third plane hitting the Pentagon and another plane crashing in a field in Pennsylvania. I was overwhelmed. I just lay there. I felt as if we were at war, and life as I knew it had ended.

As the day went on, we learned that two of the planes were American Airlines and that they both originated in Boston. One of the airlines to hit the World Trade Center that day was Flight 11, the flight where her best friend Jeff was working.

For many days after that, Rachel would call crying because she was so distraught. She wondered if she had done enough to show her friend how much she appreciated what he had done for her. She wondered what he must have been thinking and experiencing those last few moments of his life, and she played over and over again a message that he had left on her voicemail the day before he left on that fateful flight. In the voicemail, he told her he wasn't feeling well and didn't want to go to work the next day. He was considering calling in sick.

Finally, Rachel's husband had to take the phone off the hook because too many people (other flight attendants) were calling with more information on what had happened, and Rachel was overwhelmed. Jeff wasn't the only one she knew on the flight either. She had worked with every flight attendant and every pilot on both planes.

Only a few days later, I happened to be channel surfing, and I caught a conversation between Jerry Falwell and Pat Robertson. They were talking about the recent terrorist attack. I was curious about what they had to say, so I watched. Then I heard Jerry Falwell say, and I quote, "I blame the homosexuals for this."

My mouth dropped, and I stood up before the TV.

"Homosexuals?" I shouted back at the television. "Homosexuals? What the hell did we ever do to you? Every one of those terrorists was heterosexual. They were narrow-minded, Fundamentalist, woman-hating, homo-hating, freedom-suppressing, arrogant, abusive, hateful, religious zealots unable to cope with differing opinions—just like you!"

Something like that.

Unfortunately, he couldn't hear it, and all I succeeded in doing was freaking out my neighbors upstairs. I couldn't understand why in the world he would blame us. Somehow, in his mind, we had come to represent everything evil in his world. How did that happen? Why did that happen? What is it about homosexuality that he hated so vehemently? Maybe, as Shakespeare once said, "Methinks he doth protest too much." I don't know, but I know I had nothing to do with September 11. I found it as horrible and disturbing as the rest of the country. If anything, the mentality of these hijackers more closely represented his views than they did mine. As far as blame goes, it's been my experience that if you have to place blame for something, then that means three things: one, you're unable to deal with the traces of that issue in your own life—two, you're unwilling to look at your role in whatever it is you're blaming—and three, you're a judgmental jerk.

ANOTHER CHAPTER ANOTHER TWIST

In 2000, shortly after Eastside had disowned me, I wasn't sure what to do with God. On the one hand, my transition was so smooth. I was kicked out of my house only to be offered a place to live on Capitol Hill within days of being told to move. My contract with Microsoft had ended abruptly because of a class-action lawsuit filed several years earlier. Still, within a month of moving, I was gainfully employed as a content manager. I was paid to write. It was my dream job. Yet, with all that "good" going for me, I still had many "God issues," and I wasn't sure how to handle them.

A friend came to visit one day. He told me he attended a Seattle church called *The Center for Spiritual Living*. He explained a little of the philosophy, which sounded intriguing, so I attended one of the Sunday services with him. The church was, and is, part of the *Religious Science* movement (also known as *Science of Mind*, now rebranded as the *United Centers for Spiritual Living*—part of the *New Thought* movement), founded by Ernest Holmes. The philosophy was new to me. They believed that God was inside us and that It didn't care about my sexuality. They taught that all paths to God were sacred and that we were already whole and complete.

I was home. I had run away from God, only to run right back into God... only this God knew how to treat a lady.

My relationship with Sterling was my first relationship ever. I learned a lot about relationships with this man. What was most disturbing to me was how independent I was NOT. I was vulnerable, scared, and insecure, alongside a plethora of emotions I had never felt before. Looking back, I can see some codependence hanging out in the mix.

Sterling's and my seven-year relationship was turbulent. In the first place, we had two entirely differing views of God. Sterling belonged to a *"Specialty Church,"* which believed they were the only ones going to Heaven. Most churches had some form of that belief, some stronger than others. The Adventists, for example, believed that only Adventists would be allowed in Heaven, so I was used to this philosophy.

Sterling's church also believed that God would throw all homosexuals into Hell and that if there was an unrepentant homosexual in any family, that family must disown that family member. That family member would be excommunicated and not allowed contact with other church members (or God).

Against this backdrop, Sterling's and my relationship got its start and contributed to our breakup. If I thought the Seventh-day Adventist church was strict, I had just met the mother-of-all authoritarian churches. He often told me that he longed for the day God would finally accept homosexuals. I couldn't tell him I believed God already did because that would only end in a fight.

Still, it was a relationship and often rewarding. I was in love with another human being. I had someone to cuddle, hold, and share my life with (that part of my life that was safe to share with someone so afraid of God) and someone to share my body with. I was finally open.

I also think that Sterling was a narcissist... not hyperbole, but a narcissist. For one thing, he saw himself as the savior of the world. In gay parlance, he was a princess, but he also took it too far.

When we first met, he saw me as the person he wanted me to be, and as we went along, he could not handle that I wasn't the idea he fell in love with. He was always fishing for compliments and often demeaned others—even friends and family.

Sterling had a lot of gay friends, and we were always going to parties. Through him, I met a lot of gay men. That became my connection with the gay community I had been looking for. I was gay; the people around me knew I was gay, and nobody cared. The pastor at my new church knew I was gay, and she didn't care either. In fact, she loved to talk about shoes. I wasn't hiding my beach ball anymore. Sterling and I went to Gay Pride. We traveled to New York, Boston, Toronto, Vancouver, Portland, San Francisco, Chicago, Asia, and even Texas as a gay couple. My beach ball was playing happily upon the waves of this ocean of life.

Eventually, though, things fell apart, as I knew they would. I was fully aware of some deep and unhealthy aspects of Sterling's and my relationship, and I knew there wouldn't be a happy ending.

I'VE GOT GOD… RIGHT WHERE HE WANTS ME

It's been years since the breakup. Sterling has children of his own. I haven't heard from Mickey, my ex-gay mentor, since he sent me packing. Occasionally, I run into a former Exodus friend in a bar, and they tell me that they, too, gave up fighting and left the group. I don't hear from too many people from Eastside either. Thanks to Facebook, I've heard from a friend or two, but we don't discuss my new life. Other than that, it's been pretty quiet. Now that I'm "In the Deathstyle," as Mickey called it, I've lost contact with people I thought truly loved me.

On one hand, I understand this. What's happened to me since I let go of my beach ball is challenging to the Christian on so many levels. If they stayed in touch with me, the biggest challenge would be that they would have to deal with their own fear. Let's face it: homosexuality would not be such a huge issue if there wasn't so much fear and hatred mixed in, and they don't want to have to leave the comfort of their beliefs.

I've learned a few things along the way. For instance, we seem to define ourselves by our beliefs. I hear people say, "I'm a Christian," "I'm an atheist," "I'm agnostic," "I'm an alcoholic," and "I'm fed up!" Whatever it is, we place labels on ourselves, which are tags or definitions of who we think we are. We introduce ourselves based on those labels. Those beliefs take up residence in our psyche, and changing those beliefs requires us to find a new definition of ourselves. This is uncomfortable sometimes and downright painful other times.

There's one belief that goes deeper than any other. It seems to hang out very close to our Souls. That belief is our belief in God. This belief defines us. Whatever we believe about God, we believe about ourselves. This belief has greater power than any other belief we adhere to, and to take away this belief (or alter it) is to literally alter us at the very core of our being and physically change who we think we are (yes, I mean physically). I think that is why there's so much violence associated with the name of God. When you're that afraid, you have to change the world around you so that it doesn't threaten you at your deepest level.

But that's the point. If God is to be understood and loved, it must be at the deepest level of who we are. There was a time, a long time ago, when I trusted God. Somehow, I believed that he would lead me to discover myself. I believed he was okay with me challenging my beliefs, even in him. I thought God would understand that even if I were "misled," he would be compassionate because he knew I was seeking and would gently guide me back to the truth, whatever that was. I think this is what Christianity means when it talks about approaching God with a clean heart. I think this could also be what the Bible is talking about when it addresses *"stripping ourselves of false images,"* and maybe it's what Jesus meant when he said that to *"find God, you must first lose yourself."*

This isn't some platitude; this is God at Its most fundamental. And this was part of my process. The "myself" that I lost was the "myself" that I had created out of my fear and ignorance. It was also that "myself" that created the God that I knew and worshiped. What I lost was my version of God, my beliefs of what God should look like, act like, and how I should look and act in relationship to this God. The "myself" that I lost was the "myself" pretending to be me... that part of me that lives below the identity and yet thinks it is my identity.

The fifteen years I spent trying to be straight were simply fifteen years trying to defend my idol or my image of what God should look like based on certain facets that religion had created (and that I had bought into). But in the process, I met God. The God I met dwells beyond time and space, beyond the confines of the human heart, beyond the Big Bang and evolution. I met this God (though a very small part of It, to be sure) in my process of trying to accept what was happening to me as a gay man in a world that didn't allow homosexuality and spirituality to coexist...

It's been years since the breakup. Sterling has children of his own. I haven't heard from Mickey, my ex-gay mentor, since he sent me packing. Occasionally, I run into a former Exodus friend in a bar, and they tell me that they, too, gave up fighting and left the group. I don't hear from too many people from Eastside either. Thanks to Facebook, I've heard from a friend or two, but we don't discuss my new life. Other than that, it's been pretty quiet. Now that I'm "In the Deathstyle," as Mickey called it, I've lost contact with people I thought truly loved me.

On one hand, I understand this. What's happened to me since I let go of my beach ball is challenging to the Christian on so many levels. If they stayed in touch with me, the biggest challenge would be that they would have to deal with their own fear. Let's face it: homosexuality would not be such a huge issue if there wasn't so much fear and hatred mixed in, and they don't want to have to leave the comfort of their beliefs.

I've learned a few things along the way. For instance, we seem to define ourselves by our beliefs. I hear people say, "I'm a Christian," "I'm an atheist," "I'm agnostic," "I'm an alcoholic," and "I'm fed up!" Whatever it is, we place labels on ourselves, which are tags or definitions of who we think we are. We introduce ourselves based on those labels. Those beliefs take up residence in our psyche, and changing those beliefs requires us to find a new definition of ourselves. This is uncomfortable sometimes and downright painful other times.

There's one belief that goes deeper than any other. It seems to hang out very close to our Souls. That belief is our belief in God. This belief defines us. Whatever we believe about God, we believe about ourselves. This belief has greater power than any other belief we adhere to, and to take away this belief (or alter it) is to literally alter us at the very core of our being and physically change who we think we are (yes, I mean physically). I think that is why there's so much violence associated with the name of God. When you're that afraid, you have to change the world around you so that it doesn't threaten you at your deepest level.

But that's the point. If God is to be understood and loved, it must be at the deepest level of who we are. There was a time, a long time ago, when I trusted God. Somehow, I believed that he would lead me to discover myself. I believed he was okay with me challenging my beliefs, even in him. I thought God would understand that even if I were "misled," he would be compassionate because he knew I was seeking and would gently guide me back to the truth, whatever that was. I think this is what Christianity means when it talks about approaching God with a clean heart. I think this could also be what the Bible is talking about when it addresses *"stripping ourselves of false images,"* and maybe it's what Jesus meant when he said that to *"find God, you must first lose yourself."*

This isn't some platitude; this is God at Its most fundamental. And this was part of my process. The "myself" that I lost was the "myself" that I had created out of my fear and ignorance. It was also that "myself" that created the God that I knew and worshiped. What I lost was my version of God, my beliefs of what God should look like, act like, and how I should look and act in relationship to this God. The "myself" that I lost was the "myself" pretending to be me... that part of me that lives below the identity and yet thinks it is my identity.

The fifteen years I spent trying to be straight were simply fifteen years trying to defend my idol or my image of what God should look like based on certain facets that religion had created (and that I had bought into). But in the process, I met God. The God I met dwells beyond time and space, beyond the confines of the human heart, beyond the Big Bang and evolution. I met this God (though a very small part of It, to be sure) in my process of trying to accept what was happening to me as a gay man in a world that didn't allow homosexuality and spirituality to coexist...

And then I lost it.

THE LONG DARK JOURNEY INTO THE DARK SIDE OF GOD

One thing I took away from my years at Eastside was, 'I could think for myself.' The pastor firmly believed that we, as his parishioners, choose what we believe through our study, and I took that to heart. As a result, my 'relationship' with God was somewhat distinctive. As I understood it, God didn't mind if things were a little bawdy. He liked a little tequila and enjoyed a Monty Python movie. He called me toots and wasn't afraid to joke around. He was always God, but I was still allowed to relate to him more as myself and without a whole lot of religious restrictions.

But it didn't start with Eastside. If you'll recall, when I was living in Lander and later Riverton, I wanted to be a prophet, meaning I wanted to know God from my experience profoundly and powerfully that most others didn't. I wanted to know him personally. I remember hearing many times that if we were to look God in the face, we'd die instantly. But I couldn't help but think, 'What a way to go.'

I connected with God at an early age, and for whatever reason, it took. As a result, I found studying theology another way to understand God. Beyond Bible study, I could examine the reasoning behind the events and commandments. The stories made more sense, and the Bible became more fascinating.

I also started becoming more academic with my curiosity. I studied Jewish theology, culture, and history. I studied Christianity and its history. And I studied the men who allegedly wrote the Bible. At one point, I had hoped to do a college-based study and get a degree, but financially, it never worked out that I could.

That knowledge, however, led to an interesting dichotomy. As time passed, I began to understand how tenuous all this religious stuff was. I learned about the battles between the early church fathers over *acceptable doctrine.* I studied Christology and the battle over who Jesus was in relationship to God and humankind. I read about the disputes between the Jewish disciples of Jesus (led by James, the brother of Jesus) and the Gentiles (led by Paul) regarding who spoke for Jesus... and on and on and on.

All this set me up for a "Faithquake." Suddenly, I couldn't quote the Apostle's Creed with conviction as I once could. Many of the very foundations I once built my beliefs crumpled in the shakeup.

My journey into the dark side of God started with my first book, "The Warrior," published in 1995, five years before I came out—or was outed (2000). I was excited. At last, God answered my prayers, and I would be a published author. I signed the contract with the publisher in 1992, but as the years went on and the book never seemed to materialize for one reason or another, I became increasingly frustrated in the process.

At long last, the book was finally published, and I started going out and doing the things that authors do. I scheduled book signings, talks, and other events to corroborate the book, but I would show up at the book signing only to learn that the bookstore couldn't get the book. Slowly, things began to unravel. I then learned that the government raided the publisher and was brought up on serious charges, not the least of which was embezzlement. On top of that, they owned the rights to my book.

I contacted an attorney who was recommended to me by a friend. She helped people in situations like mine and took on the case. She fought hard and got my rights back for me. In the end, she only charged me fifty dollars. The rights were now mine, but the book wasn't. They had printed a thousand, and I had no claim to them because of the bankruptcy.

The attorneys set it up so that the authors would have to bid on their own books. But before anyone had that chance, a single entrepreneur outbid all the authors. He could do so because he could buy all the books at once, and the courts felt this was better. So every author with this company lost their books. I shouldn't say "lost." This man bought the books for about fifty cents apiece and then tried to sell them back to the authors for much more. In my case, he tried to sell my books back to me at three dollars per book. When I told him I could not afford the books, he responded that I would make it back when I sold them. I reminded him that selling books wouldn't be that easy with no distribution, marketing, or support behind me. So the books were gone.

Why would I be so challenged over this? Most of it was because writing was another big dream. After so many years, it seemed as if God was finally allowing me an opportunity to fulfill one of my dreams, only to let it all fall apart. Did God look into my future and determine that I wasn't ready? I couldn't get the nagging feeling out of my mind that I was never going to overcome my sexuality issues, and therefore, God was never going to allow me to live out my dreams. Instead, he would dangle them over me like a carrot while I spent my whole life in complete futility. I was crushed. At this point, I began to consider that maybe things were never going to turn around for me, and perhaps it wasn't worth trying.

It was another one of those moments when I wondered if it was even worth being on the planet. So, again, I started to consider my "options seriously." How could I best get off this ball of dirt with the least amount of pain, and did I have the courage to do so?

As I considered this, I continued to go back to what my mom went through when Brian died and how much that tore her up. I remember watching how she suffered losing her son, and I begged God often that she would never have to suffer like that again.

Then, one day, I thought, "She'll get over it. After all, it's not that far down the road when she'll join me."

It was at that moment that I realized I was in trouble. I had never been so despondent, so I started researching the easiest ways to check out. In the midst of this, a voice, probably stronger than I've ever experienced, began to resonate in my head. It wasn't a one-time thing; it was more like a "nagging" question asked repeatedly, and I mean nagging. The question continued to nag me incessantly, and I couldn't shut it up.

"What if the Buddha is right?" The question started off. "What if you have to keep coming back until you get it right?"

It's hard to describe all the feelings, thoughts, and emotions that swirled around this question. It would take pages and pages to write what I experienced in only the length of time it took to write the question. What it eventually boiled down to, though, was that I did not want to return and do it again. The thought of that was so distressing, even more so than the thought that I couldn't last another day with the anguish that had, at this point, consumed me. So I did the next best thing. I took a trip to the doctor, and I got myself on antidepressants.

It was obvious that God and I weren't going to be able to reconcile, but I wasn't ready to leave him yet, so to cope with these feelings, I took my deceased grandfather's wedding ring and put it on my wedding finger. I considered this a difficult time in my relationship with God. Still, it was a relationship I planned to have forever, and the ring would remind me that I was still in this relationship.

1995 turned out to be a challenging year for many of my friends.

I wasn't the only one of my friends suddenly hurled into the throws of this Godforsaken (literally) barren wasteland.

My close friend Jordon had a girlfriend he loved deeply. One night while at a party, Jordan's girlfriend was raped. Not only did her attacker violate her physically and psychologically, but he also left her with a permanent reminder of his assault. He gave her his STDs. These diseases, in turn, left her with some serious health problems.

The first time Jordon told me about it was the first time I had ever seen him get emotional about anything, and this was gut-wrenching. He sobbed so hard that his body shook. His agony was so profound that I was overwhelmed just listening to it. I couldn't imagine what this must have felt like.

Not knowing what else to do, I listened to him as he told me the story.

For many days after that, we would meet, cry, pray, and beg God to help us understand why our lives were in such disarray.

My other friend Bobby was having problems of his own.

Bobby was suffering from severe neurological issues, and he was nearly bedridden most of the time. Doctors ran every test available but couldn't figure out what was wrong. Sometimes, his whole body was just one heap of aching, throbbing agony. There were days he couldn't even get out of bed to defecate.

He, too, was praying, begging God for healing. He went from being healthy to losing total control of his life.

So there were three of us, all struggling with serious God issues. In Bobby's case, it was his health. In Jordan's case, it was his girlfriend. In my case, it was my dreams (wrapped up in my sexuality). In all of our cases, it was abandonment. Where was God when we so desperately needed him?

Our trauma besieged us, and we struggled over what to do with ourselves, each other, and God. During this bizarre period of our lives, we had to rethink God and what we would do as Christians.

In my case, during this whole period, another thing kept running through my head. It was that night back at Eastside and Kyle Martin's proclamation, "You're not gay." Jordan and I talked at length about what that must mean, but despite years of therapy, the focus on prayer, and life with Exodus, there wasn't any truth to Kyle's declaration.

I stopped referring to God as God and started referring to him as "The Universe" or "Cosmic Intelligence" (if there was such a thing out there in the universe), but ultimately, deep down inside, I felt that if God did exist, he didn't give a sh!t about me. So I wouldn't give a sh!t about him either. But I never took off the wedding ring because I also hoped that I was wrong and that God did give a sh!t about me and that one day he would at least attempt to show me so. That's how I handled this crisis.

Bobby, on the other hand, took the scientific approach. He returned to science and decided that atheism was the best solution to his problem. The universe was far too random, and if there was a God, he didn't have a handle on things. He decided that life was what it was. It had a beginning and an end, and everything in between was pure chance.

On the other hand, Jordan figured that maybe God didn't have as much control over the universe as we were taught as Christians and that maybe our purpose in life was to cope. He pontificated that maybe God was as helpless as we were in the face of suffering.

So there we were, the three of us falling apart and suffering from the collapse of our spiritual infrastructure resulting from our so-called Faithquakes.

Jordan heard about a therapist in Florida who was supposed to be good. Before we knew it, we were on a plane headed for Daytona Beach (actually, it was Seattle to Atlanta, then Atlanta to Orlando—from there, we drove to Daytona). What's a little more therapy in the scope of all that I have been through so far? Besides, who could pass up a trip to Daytona Beach, Florida?

However, aside from a fantastic two-week vacation, neither Jordan nor I felt it had done us any good. So, we returned to Seattle to live with our predicaments. We each handled our Faithquake differently, but we did try to rebuild. Eventually, Bobby stopped worrying about science and decided that God was God, and the Bible was truth, not science. Jordan started a Web site where he took on the issues between science and God. He became an expert on many issues centered on this debate.

Me? Well, you just read my story. I managed to hang in there for a few more years, but things were changing radically. After this Faithquake, I rebuilt too, but the foundation had shifted. I paid close attention to my conversations with Bobby and Jordan regarding our challenges while trying to reconcile God, science, the real world, and our own lives.

Fast-forward to 2000, after the outing and my introduction to The Center for Spiritual Living, God took on another form. In my Christian experience, God was always a father... they called him a loving father, but he looked an awful lot like an alcoholic father. When he was sober, he was faithful, just, gentle, and loving, but when he was drunk, *he thundered through the heavens without pity and swallowed up all the dwellings of Jacob. In his wrath, he has torn down the strongholds of the daughter of Judah.* Regardless of how good he was supposed to be, no matter what he was doing for his children at every point in the Bible, there was always that undercurrent of violence.

The story of Jesus perpetuates this! God could not look upon sin, so he sent his son to stand in our place. To that end, Jesus was tortured and beaten and "endured the wrath of God." According to Paul, God still couldn't look upon us even after it was over. Instead, he sees Jesus instead of us. So, even in the New Testament, the undercurrent of violence is ever-present.

I like to refer to Jesus as 'God Light!'

As relationships go, a relationship with Jesus Christ is more dysfunctional than most of the relationships my gay friends came out of. It starts out that you either accepted Jesus as your personal savior or he will sick his father on you. If Jesus can't have you, then nobody can. If you choose not to accept Jesus Christ as your personal savior, he becomes a stalker, and you've all heard this prayer, "Do whatever it takes to get them saved."

It's even more incongruous that those who are virulently anti-gay use the metaphor of Jesus as a lover. Paul said that in the presence of God, Jesus is the groom, and we are the bride.

I realize it looks like I'm being snarky and prone to hyperbolism, but this is the backdrop with which God has been viewed historically, even though we haven't been aware. While we've spoken openly of a loving God, we are subconsciously aware of the violent backdrop with which God operates. Most apologists have had difficulty reconciling these two extremes, and we subconsciously have that same problem. It continues to go unresolved until we deal with this, and we take it out on each other.

When I walked into The Center for Spiritual Living, this version of God was not present.

I was already whole and complete in God's eyes. God saw me as an expression of life, and God loved life and supported it with Its whole existence. God was the Universe itself, and I was merely an expression of that. As an expression of God, everything I desired was God's will. God was already predetermined to give me anything I asked. There were specific universal laws, and they always worked. If I followed them, they would always work for me. If I choose not to have anything to do with God, God still wouldn't care. This God had only one rule: Harm no one. If it brought life to you and those around you, then that was God.

This meant I didn't have to beg God for anything as I had to do as a Christian. I didn't have to hope that my desire was "God's will." I didn't have to fear that I would never succeed as long as I was gay. If I wanted to be a writer, I could be a writer. If I wanted to be a gay writer, I could be a gay writer. If I wanted to write about gay issues with God in the middle of it, I could. God wasn't the insecure father who needed me to worship, adore, and do everything his way constantly. God hung out with me and considered me just like Itself.

While this sounds too good to be true, I struggled to get my head around that. Of course, I could recognize it intellectually, but it was a different story when putting it into practice. The God of my youth was indelibly burned into my psyche.

Good or bad, with the God I had just left, I had "pictures" of him. I had images of him, ideas of him, concepts of him, some good, some bad, but I had something there that I could use to orient myself to God. This new God did not have any visuals. I had no reference point. So, the God I knew continued to overshadow the God I wanted to know.

The relationship dynamics with my new God seemed to be the same. Where was God? Why did God abandon me? Only this was much harder since God had ceased to be my father. That image, that anchor, was gone. Now, it was just an entity with which I had nothing in common. I couldn't relate to an entity without a personality I could not anthropomorphize. God was neither here nor there. It was a non-entity within creation somehow. I could never wrap my head around that, and I wondered if God and I would ever come together.

Then it happened. I was sitting in church one day, and through that weird association process, the word 'agnostic' shot through my head. Maybe I was agnostic. As I left the service, as I often do, I prayed and talked to God about what I experienced during that particular service. On the way home this Sunday, my prayer was, "God, I get it—I'm agnostic. I don't know if I believe in you or not." Then I laughed at the joke of me praying to a God I wasn't sure I believed in.

THE GIFT OF ZHAN AND THE NEEDLESS FIASCO

The year was 2007. My partner and I had just broken up, and I was still attending the Center for Spiritual Living. I was sitting comfortably, meditating, and my mind took me back to Billings, Montana, and the events that involved Zhan and Calvin. Since they presented themselves so strongly, I decided to sit with them for a while.

These were difficult memories because I returned to Zhan and Calvin and that whole fiasco. I decided that maybe it was time to take these events and feelings "into God's light" and seek forgiveness for my part, especially regarding Calvin. As I was going through my forgiveness process, something profound happened. I got a strong sense of that place in Billings. The feelings, the emotions, it was all clear, as if I were there again. Then I remembered being with Zhan, how we got along for the short time we were together, and suddenly realized, "Zhan was a gift." That's right, Zhan was a gift from the Universe, and I misunderstood. In all my ranting and raving and my crazy guilt, I missed it.

This wasn't a moment of condemnation for me, though, nor was it meant to make me feel regret. It was an opportunity for me to recognize that, as a human being, I tend to operate only out of my beliefs, which often have little to do with reality. I let a belief turn a blessing into a curse, and I didn't even know it. So, I blessed Zhan and thanked him for being willing to participate in this lesson.

I then took Calvin into the light. I asked that he forgive me and asked that, hopefully, someday, he will understand what I was going through and that it was never against him. I also asked God to bless Calvin and give him that break he deserved.

ANOTHER LETTER TO DAD

By now, we were almost a decade into the new century. Sterling and I had been separated for nearly two years. A friend from my church introduced me to Landmark Education, a hard-core, three-day program that " gives you the skills" to change your life. I signed up based on her recommendation and took the class. It was Friday through Sunday, from ten in the morning to ten at night.

I sat in a chair for three days and listened to the lecturer speak. By Friday evening, I had already started to feel some strong resistance to the instructor. By Saturday, I realized that I didn't like this guy at all. He seemed abrasive, obnoxious, and dismissive of others' opinions. I couldn't understand why I felt like that. So, I started searching my psyche for any understanding of this conflict.

On Saturday, we were coming up on a half-hour break, and the instructor gave us an assignment to do over the break. That assignment was to write a letter to someone we needed to clean things up with. I assumed that my issue with this speaker must be related to an unknown issue with my dad. So, I decided that's who I would write my letter to. I would write another letter to my father since there must still be things I needed to clean up. I had no intention of mailing this letter since I had already told him how I felt. There wasn't any reason to take that further. I was merely trying to clear things up with myself.

However, as I wrote the letter, I realized things had shifted, and I was okay with my dad. I found this surprising, but since I started the letter, I decided to go ahead and finish it. I told my dad in the letter that, as far as I was concerned, we were okay. There was no longer anything between us. In the letter, I explained to him that I wasn't looking for a relationship and didn't need anything from him. I was letting everything between us go. The reason, I told him, for the letter was so that he and I would no longer be "entangled." We could move on, each one with our own lives. By the time I was done with the letter, I decided to go ahead and send it.

Why not?

I heard back from him. He acknowledged that we were clean and reaffirmed that he would never apologize for what he did. At first, that made me angry, so I took that one into my forgiveness process and let it go.

It did not, however, help me feel better about my instructor. So, when the class was over, I took what I had learned and let the rest go.

THE MORAL OF THE STORY

I've often said, "Since I gave up on God, I feel much better about him." As I walked through all of this God-confusion, I had no idea what was happening to me and in me was healthy. I was a two-year-old/teenager learning to assert my independence. In the process of giving up on God, I started to learn how to think for myself and stop relying on someone or something for everything I wanted my life to be. This also meant that I started learning not to blame anyone else when my life didn't go as I wanted.

I started to learn that I was the driver of my life, not the passenger, and God was the car. God was the vehicle through which my life was lived, but I was the life and body, and it was up to me to move the car to wherever my chosen destination would be. God would carry me.

As I said earlier, our beliefs about God are as close to our identity as possible. Therefore, whatever we believe about ourselves, we believe about God at a deep level, and whatever we believe about God, we believe about ourselves. My journey away from Christianity was not a journey away from God, though it initially looked that way. It challenged me to look beyond my beliefs and into the Universe and give up my definition of God. In spiritual terms, I believe that's what it means to "die to ourselves" or to "take up our cross." The reality was that the "Father" that I missed so profoundly wasn't God; it was something that I created to make up for my deficit of what I thought a father should be. Since the image I had of God was an image that I created, it was only natural that this image would change as I changed, and it was especially natural that as God disappeared, I would find myself feeling lost and alone.

This sounds "scholastic" and "reasonable," but it's pretty much BS.

As I said earlier, the story begins and ends with God. I only had a problem with this issue because God had a problem with it. Had God been okay with it, I would have continued to do most of the things

I had already been doing: praying, seeking a deeper relationship with him, writing songs, and connecting with others. And I would do them without the fear that something was standing between us.

And I can pretend that I walked away with a new understanding of God—an open and compassionate understanding. But that would be a lie. I don't understand him/it at all. I could pretend that I walked out of this morass a stronger person. But I didn't. I was broken. I've spent a considerable portion of my life trying to recover some semblance of order, only to lose myself in the chaos of life.

But there was one thing I knew for sure. God, whatever that was, didn't hate me. It had no problem with my sexuality. It didn't play that horrific joke on me by making me gay and then forcing me to change. And that was enough to take a massive weight off my shoulders.

Since I started questioning God and his relationship with me, I have been unable to find a place where I can relate in any genuine way. Where I once saw compassion, I see darkness. Where I once saw hope, I see darkness. I'm often accused of hating God, so I've become an atheist. My response to that is, first of all, I'm not an atheist, and second, hating God is like hating Santa Claus. It's a complete waste of hate since neither one of them exists.

Or do they?

The one thing that became abundantly clear through this struggle was that the God I had created this beautiful relationship with—was me. I was the entity who liked Monty Python, tequila, and chasing men. I was the entity that called me toots, and I was the entity that saw beyond the hate that prevailed in so many of my religious experiences. In a weird sort of way... I was God.

You'd think I'd be happy about that. Instead, I was devastated. Of all the people I could trust, I was the most untrustworthy. I needed a force outside of me that accepted and loved me and helped me cope with life's challenges. And those people came to me... not because of God, but because of my sincerity. I had to learn that I needed my community—not one that only offered "thoughts and prayers," but one that cared for themselves and each other. That was as close to God as I would get—at least for now.

Early in our development, our species created stories that would forever determine the direction of the human race... the stories of gods. We left the savannas of Africa with the need to worship and bow to beings bigger than us. And tens of thousands of years later, that hasn't changed.

Yet why would I say that these stories of God were true?

Every year, around late November or early December, we tell stories of an aged fat man who rides in a sleigh and brings happiness to children around the world, both young and old. Does Santa exist? Of course not. But yet, he does. Santa exists because we created him. Every year, we give great emotional fortitude to this being who brings happiness and joy. Santa, of course, is tied in with the story of Jesus, the baby who came to earth to rescue the suffering humans and restore to them everything they were meant to be.

These stories have been told over and over and over again for thousands of years. And they have grown, expanded, and changed throughout the years. But most importantly, they have become more ingrained in the human psyche.

Harry Potter. This story has captivated the imagination of young and old alike. J.R.R. Tolkien's Lord of the Rings trilogy has also captivated the human soul. These stories, though they are fiction, exist. They exist because we gave them life and continue to do so.

The God that we currently understand is very much story-based. He originates from El... the Sumerian God, many years before Yahweh. In Sumerian times, El is depicted as an old man with a long flowing beard and white hair. (Sound familiar?)

Whether or not God exists that's a different story. There is, or at least seems to be, an intelligence in the universe. Does that mean that intelligence can relate to humans? Maybe not. Maybe the God we talk about doesn't speak human because it's bigger than all that. The problem is, we'll never get out of this place to determine whether that's true. So what do we do? We need to create a God that makes sense. A God that looks like us, though not like El.

If you read the Bible, our stories about God, and especially our stories about Jesus, you will see that what we're looking for is the best in ourselves. We use Jesus and God to help us overcome our weaknesses and aspire to the things we know we can attain. Other religions use Allah, Buddha (who is not a God), Jesus (the Son of God), Ganesha (the God of gods), Zeus, Odin... So, the Gods already exist.

What we need to do, then, since we already have the template, is to create a God who represents the best of us and who can help us achieve the best of us. And that won't be easy because we don't even know who we are or what we're capable of.

And this is where I landed with God. I cannot explain the devastation, the near destruction of everything I held sacred. For a while, I had something I thought I could trust; I could love who would care for me and help me become the person I wanted to be. And then that person vanished in a puff of smoke. And here I was, lost, alone, abandoned. There's no way to describe those feelings. There is no way to explain those feelings. Only that they were there, and I had no choice but to experience them whether I wanted to or not. The closest analogy is a breakup with the most crucial person in your life.

My relationship with God took a massive hit during that time of discovery, where I learned that I would never be straight or change who I was at this fundamental level. I remember one day, sitting in my prayer room, a room in my house that I had dedicated specifically to praying. I plead with God, "Please, God. Please show me something. Show me you're remotely interested. Do something. In the process of that prayer, I became so sexually turned on that I felt like I was about to orgasm. What the hell?

This was it. God, as I understood him, was not God as I understood him. I hate chaos. And yet chaos is everywhere, and the God I believed in could do nothing to prevent that. He was good at giving me ideas, pep talks, and helping me work out things. All things that I could do. But he wasn't able to work beyond me.

What do I do? How do I avoid this chaos?

In 2014, I would make two more moves. Long distance from Seattle to New Windsor in Upstate New York and then to Suffern, on the other side of the Hudson from Manhattan. Now we're at 32.

In July 2017, my brother-in-law, a loadmaster on the KC130, was flying over Mississippi at a cruising altitude of 30,000 feet when a catastrophic malfunction occurred. One of the propellers on the plane's left wing came loose and flew through the body, bending the fuselage and cutting the plane in half. The plane broke into pieces over a seven-mile swath of soy fields. Sixteen military men lost their lives. Fifteen Marines and one Navy corpsman who was hitching a ride. One of those marines was my brother-in-law, Brendan Johnson.

I was flipping channels on T.V. that day, looking for something worth watching. I landed on CNN and saw the accident. There were images of debris and fires burning the fields of what looked to be a sparsely populated area. Listening to the commentators, I determined it wasn't Brendan's plane. Two planes were flying that day, each starting from the same area but taking different routes to their location. I quickly texted my brother-in-law, "Brendan, are you okay?" thinking I would get a reply within an hour or so.

I flipped to another channel, less newsy; all the while, in the back of my head, I couldn't help but wonder. An hour came and went, and I didn't get a response. Now I was worried.

That night, around 9:00 PM, my sister called. Rachel was still with the airlines, only now she was a union rep for LaGuardia/JFK airports. She had been in Texas for meetings and called me. She broke the news that the plane that crashed was Brendan's plane. My surrogate *little brother* had been killed in a catastrophic failure (that's what the report called it). You might call it "two for two."

For the next two months, we would deal with military protocol in many ways we didn't even know was possible. We wanted to bury him in Arlington Cemetery, which was books worth of paperwork. But because of the nature of the accident, there were a lot of protocols to fulfill. A memorial service was planned at the base where Brendan was stationed. After that, a service was planned for Brendan's New York brothers at a funeral home in Fishkill, where he lived. Military personnel came from around the state to say goodbye.

After that, Brendan's body... or at least what was left after the fire, was taken down to Arlington, where he would be laid to rest. Hundreds of Marines stood behind the family at this funeral as the service progressed. It was indeed one of the most somber services I had ever experienced.

Of course, the president at the time never spoke of it, aside from a tweet, and was actively hostile toward one of the widows... Rachel. She dared to ask him to say something... anything... about what had happened. It took the Senator of Vermont (Bernie Sanders—Brendan's parents lived in Vermont, and they went to him) and the Senator of New York (Chuck Schumer—Brendan was stationed in New Windsor, New York) to finally get Rachel a letter of recognition for her husband's service to our country.

I used to joke with Brendan that he was my "little brother." Well, now that joke wasn't going to work anymore.

Ironically, during the memorials and the services and grieving, we experienced the very worst of Evangelical behavior. What would follow was disparaging remarks and hundreds of letters from people who didn't know her or Brendan telling her that this event happened because neither of them knew Christ—or somehow rejected him. How could these strangers know what was happening in my sister's and her husband's lives, especially something so personal as their relationship with Christ?

The answer is they were just making shit up. But that's the problem. God, whoever it was, could not or would not control its people. And it led them to do so much damage to grieving people. This is something we see often. There isn't a painful place that they can't make even more painful.

Rachel gave an interview with Guts and Glory, Dan Rather's website. The comments that came from that were so brutal that it was difficult to read. To be clear, there were beautiful, supportive comments. But the religious people, those who claimed to have a unique knowledge of God, we're fucking brutal. They said the vilest, ugly things, such as, "What does she want? Does she want the country to wipe her little ass for her?" She never said that at all, and we, as a nation, promised we'd take care of these people and their families.

I look into the future and don't know what I see. When I die, will I be at peace, will I die and see nothing, or will I have a moment where I stand in the presence of a being who has the answers to all this stuff? I don't know. I wish I did. However, I find myself living as if both of those possibilities are true. I will die, cease to exist, and not remember anything else; I will be gone. Or I will finally find a place where the answers will be provided, and I will finally understand what the fuck is going on. Since no one has ever died and come back, we can only speculate.

We live in a universe that suffers greatly. We see it as galaxies colliding, as black holes swallow stars and planets. It's ever-present. And at no point do there seem to be any answers forthcoming as to why.

As I've said many times, I feel much better about God since I gave up on him. In that place, I think I can finally be free enough to let whatever it is in life just be what it is.

TRUTH WILL WIN OUT

I look back on this book, and it got longer than I had initially anticipated, and now, instead of being done, I realize there's still a little more I must address, or this manuscript will be incomplete to me.

I strongly resisted jumping into the fray and addressing the arguments around this issue, especially regarding homosexuality and the Bible. For one thing, there's very little I can say that hasn't already been said before. Many people are already explaining the spiritual/ Biblical issues of homosexuality. Still, I feel that talking about them will open up the challenges we face from our Christian friends and from those who are determined that they are going to do everything in their power to make sure that gay men and women are never allowed to be who they are.

The only apparent reason that Christians have to disapprove of homosexuality is based on one book... the Bible, although, in all fairness, the Bible is a collection of many books that have been edited together over centuries and millennia. It includes history, poetry, legal codes, mythologies, commentary, letters, sayings, and songs. It's also divided into two testaments: the Old Testament and the New Testament.

There's no scientific evidence that homosexuality is wrong, no psychological or physiological evidence that it's wrong, and we don't see anything in nature that makes it wrong. It's just this one tome. That there is prejudice and bias against homosexuals is without question. We've been tribal for thousands of years, and there has always been prejudice against minority groups and those that aren't in our tribe. Still, it's through the Bible that many anti-gay groups go after homosexuality. They can take this book and use it as a basis for their prejudice, and they don't have to be accountable for their intolerance.

When discussing the issue, my detractor first tells me, "The Bible condemns it." My response to that is, "So?" The Bhagavad Gita doesn't address it at all. The Upanishads and the Vedas don't seem to address it, and the Talmud doesn't record a single instance of anyone being brought up on charges of homosexuality.

Yes, the Bible condemns it in a few instances (and I will cover those later), as does the Qur'an. But the Qur'an does not bind me, and the Bible does not bind me. I don't believe in the Bible the way Christians believe in the Bible. That's their point of view, not mine, and therefore I shouldn't be judged by their beliefs. The Bible is not a scientific book; it's neither a historical nor a psychological book.

That argument, however, doesn't help many gay men and women because, at a very deep level, they do believe in the Bible. It also doesn't mean anything to the Christians who believe at a very deep level that I do need to believe the way they do and that it's their responsibility to convince me or bring me around to their point of view—and if they can't do so by reason, then they must do so by force. I'm standing in what might be considered 'No Man's Land.' On the one hand, I'm watching people struggling desperately to reconcile their God and their sexuality. On the other hand, the Christians are trying desperately to influence their viewpoint onto me and those of us who don't see life the way they do.

So that's why I jumped into the fray, because of everything I've been through up to this point, all in an attempt to serve God as fully as possible. I'm no longer at that place where spirituality or God can be so narrowly defined. That belief—or cloud, if you will—has sailed on.

It's one of the Christian's favorite mantras, and they intone it in their best James Dobson voice. "It's against nature."

Well, it's against nature for us to wear clothes. It's against nature for us to use a toilet instead of doing what the animals do. Where do animals go to the bathroom? Wherever they have to, whenever they feel the urge. It's against nature to get into a machine made of tin and drive it down the road at 60 to 80 miles an hour. It's against nature to build buildings into the clouds. It's against nature to get into a 60-ton machine and hurl yourself through the air thirty-thousand feet off the ground, at 600 miles per. It's against nature to marry one person and live with that person for the rest of your life (do you know of any animals that do that?). It's against nature to watch HBO and eat Ho-Hos. It's against nature to go into a person and cut away a cancer cell with light; it's against nature to get pregnant using artificial methods when it's already been shown that you can't have children. We don't do all these things naturally, so why is it okay to do them now? The fact that we're human means we can live "beyond nature." We are the only creatures on earth to be given the ability to reason, think, and hold ourselves accountable for our actions. We are the only creatures who can manipulate our environment with such energy.

That's part of what makes us unique. Humans can do things that may not be in our nature, such as fly in airplanes and send men to the moon. If you look at the animal kingdom (as many Christians want to do in trying to prove that nature doesn't behave this way), you will also find that many animals don't have families. Most animals mate, and then the male of the species disappears, and the mother is left to fend for herself. In some species, the mother disappears soon after the young are born or hatched. Some mothers eat their young; some animals prey on other animals.

Not every sheep is born white. Some white cats have black spots. Some black cats have white spots. Wolves have very distinctive patterns. Trees and plants have different patterns. That's natural. The fact that some people would be gay or lesbian is a testament to nature and her love for diversity. Nothing in nature looks one hundred percent like its counterpart, even at its most basic structure, the DNA.

I've often wondered if maybe homosexuality wasn't nature's way of slowing down the population so that she could guarantee enough room for everybody. As the old Jewish saying goes, "God makes more people, but he doesn't make more land," and right now, with the planet's population expanding exponentially, aside from a major disaster, this is how nature will have to slow the population. It would be more drastic and violent if she had to do it another way. I prefer this way. So, in that sense, we may even be saving the planet.

The biggest argument is probably the Adam and Eve debate. "In the beginning, God created Adam and Eve, not Adam and Steve."

In Seattle, where I live, there's been what I call "the Fish Wars." It started with the Jesus fish on the back of many cars. Then someone took this fish and added legs to it, and inside the fish, inserted the word "Darwin." Then someone got a Jesus fish and showed it eating the Darwin fish. Then I saw a Darwin fish humping the Jesus fish. My favorite was the fish that used the Jesus fish symbol, but inside, it said, "N' Chips." Now Christians have the fish with the word "Truth" written inside eating the Darwin fish.

What amazes me most about this fish is the word "Truth." In our generation, as science has changed our world (and our view of the world), one group still refuses to deal with the truth. Why is that? The one group of people that should care most about the truth (and says they care most about the truth) is the one group of people that will go to the most extraordinary lengths to avoid it or to try to change it while they continue to claim that they "have" the truth. I've discovered that when they speak the truth, they talk about dogma. They have labeled their "dogma" as truth.

I don't argue it much anymore because it isn't worth it. No matter how the evidence piles up, a group of people are determined to disprove and refute that evidence. If this evidence could be discredited, I would say, "Great!" It would be easier for me to point to Eden and say, "That's my heritage." That would solve many of my problems. I'd have a purpose, a reason for being. I'd have a connection with God.

I remember watching an interview with conspiracy theorists who believed that the first NASA trip to the moon was a hoax. You've probably heard that a few times. They interviewed one man, and he told the interviewer there was no way they could make him believe otherwise. That's when it hit me. Truth wasn't an issue for him. He had decided that he would never believe, and therefore, he would never allow anything to challenge that belief. The same is true in this debate. This isn't a logical debate; it's an emotional debate. Creationists want this to be true and try to make it accurate, whether it is or not.

I've had this conversation so many times. The last time went something like this: I was talking with a girl one day on Capitol Hill who was proselytizing, trying to convert some homos (they like to come to Capitol Hill), and we were discussing the Adam and Eve scenario. That's when I told her what I'm telling you, what I believe about the evolution of our planet.

"Okay," was her response, "then where did the ape come from?"

Knowing where she was going from my own fifteen years as a Christian, I decided to play along with her just for fun.

"And where did the primordial goo come from?" she continued.

I talked about the idea of a "singularity." While it's been called a Big Bang, I've heard there wasn't necessarily a 'bang' though I'm not a physicist; I just read about it. The best I could say was that our Universe started as an infinitesimally small, infinitely hot, and dense... singularity.

She hadn't heard that one, but she powered on undaunted. "And where did that singularity(?) come from?" she asked. She was confused about what the word meant but now had a smug smile. She thought she had me. In her mind, something had to start the whole thing rolling.

But that's when I asked her— "And where did God come from?"

Her answer: "Well, he always was."

"But that doesn't make sense," I responded.

"But he's God," she said, wondering why I wasn't seeing this elementary and straightforward logic.

Then I said— "If it's easy to believe that God just was and that he's always been, isn't it just as easy to believe that the universe just was and always was? If something can't come from nothing, then even

God could not have come from nothing. Creation is an outside event, meaning it took place outside the Universe, yet there isn't anything outside the Universe. Therefore, God must be embedded inside the Universe somewhere."

Now she was angry. "You have to believe in God! Everything has to start from something. You said it yourself: A singularity created the universe. Something started it."

"Well then," I asked. "Isn't it possible that that same event created God? Perhaps they both arrived together."

The discussion was over. I was rebuked in the name of Jesus and condemned to burn in hell for all eternity for not believing in a loving God who wants me to be with him for eternity but on his terms—or else.

I sometimes wonder if maybe God is beyond all time. Maybe God wasn't "in the beginning," maybe God was "from the beginning": A small but radically significant difference. When we look at God, we are looking at something beyond all that is, yet exists within all that is. That means our experience with God can only be personal and happen within our connection to the Universe. I cannot tell you how to experience God, and you cannot tell me.

The evolution debate is genuinely at the crux of the anti-gay movement. When we finally put the evolution debate to rest, we will finally be able to discuss the gay issue logically and scientifically. The only way the anti-gay movement can justify their prejudice is based on the story of Adam and Eve. Their belief that God created man and woman justifies their intolerance of anything that doesn't fit that template. That's why they hang on so tightly to the creation story.

Rational beings find themselves confused. Why do Fundamentalists fight so hard against a proven scientific reality? Why do they risk looking unintelligible and illiterate in the face of science? I think the answer is fear, and it's wrapped up in the Creation story itself.

Since there's no way we can know everything, we create beliefs about it to cope with this uncertainty. These beliefs are built to orient us in this giant cacophony we call a Universe and to help us localize the infinite so that there's something we can call "real." We build our beliefs through generalization, deletion, and distortion. We take the millions of bits of information coming at us every second, generalize what we can, and delete what we can't, which creates distortion. A song on the radio is a perfect example of this effect. The song comprises instruments such as drums, guitars, bass, keyboards, vocals, and background vocals... It's then arranged, recorded, and mixed before it reaches our music device. However, all we hear is the song, a generalized sound.

So, from the onset, our beliefs pose a problem. They're not built on reality. They're built upon our perception of reality. Ironically, once a belief is in place, it begins to regulate our reality, filtering everything that disagrees with it and only letting in what supports it, even if this is a painful or destructive belief. As beliefs grow, they take up more space in our psyche, and we forget that the Universe is happening despite our belief about it.

When Charles Darwin published "Origin of the Species" in 1859, Christianity struggled with and separated itself from science. Darwin didn't create the Theory of Evolution and went to great lengths in his book to credit others who had said it before him, but like it or not, history calls him the "Father of Evolution." His so-called "theory" goes to the very heart of the belief system that Christianity was built on.

Creationism answered our fundamental questions: Why are we here? What is our purpose in life, why is there suffering, what happens after we die, and how will it all end?

First Question: "Why are we here?"

According to the first creation story in Genesis, God felt creative, so he spent a five-day-work-week creating our world and its supporting Universe. On the sixth day, he crowned his new world with his most excellent conception... the human being. (In some Christian mythologies, the creation of man prompted Lucifer's rebellion.) In the first creation story, it was the human male; in the second, it was male and female. The story doesn't necessarily say WHY God created humankind, but it does say that God DID, and that's enough for most Fundamentalists. We're here because God created us. This gives us our place in the Universe and establishes our purpose.

Second Question: What is our Purpose in Life?

This question is shakier regarding answers, but it's still answered in the creation story. Once God was finished with his humans, he put them in a garden and gave them dominion over all the Earth. So, "technically," our purpose is to serve God, act as his surrogate on Earth, and "be his gardeners." Christian texts later suggested our sole purpose is to "worship and praise God." They didn't tell us how to do that per se, but that did give us a purpose and, equally as important, a connection to this thing called our Source.

Third Question: Why is there pain and suffering in the world?

Human suffering and its reasons are the most discussed topic on Earth, and it's the only question that we'll openly debate with the parameters of God still in the framework. It's in all of our religious doctrines, it's in our newspapers, and it even shows up to varying degrees in our school textbooks. We're profoundly troubled by human suffering, which makes the creation story much more powerful. God wanted to give humankind "Free Will." To do that, he put a tree in the middle of his Garden and called it the Tree of the Knowledge of Good and Evil. He told Adam and Eve that of all the trees in the garden, they could not eat from this tree. Naturally, if you tell a kid NOT to do something, that's the first thing they will do. So, Eve, then Adam, disobeyed God's direct order and was ejected from the Garden. God told Eve that she would bear children in pain. God told Adam that the Earth would bear fruit only by the sweat of his brow. Viola, we now know why there's pain and suffering. The Apostle Paul would develop a doctrine around this when he created Christianity.

Fourth Question: When will it all end?

This question requires knowledge of both New and Old Testaments. It also requires some insight into both Judaism and Christianity. Let's start with Judaism since it was their text in the first place. According to Judaic texts, complete compliance with God's laws would become necessary for human salvation. There are 613 Laws in the Torah, 365 negative and 248 positive, and, according to the Jewish teachers, God restored Israel only when they were all obeyed by all of Israel.

Christianity took this and created a new doctrine in the person of Yeshua (Joshua) or Jesus—in Greek, the Christ. In the Pauline story, one man, Adam, sinned in the Garden of Eden, bringing death to the world. God knew there was no way a man would ever keep every jot and tittle of these 613 laws that he handed down to Moses, so he sent his son. Jesus embodied the law and then became that "sacrificial lamb" and took on the full wrath of God and our punishment by dying for our sins. We are no longer bound to the law but forgiven through his Sacrifice. Thanks to Jesus, there is no need for suffering. Soon, Jesus will return and take all those who accepted him as their savior, and it will all be over.

We don't have an official date for the destruction of humankind, but we know it's close, and we can anticipate it with great expectation.

Fifth Question: What happens after we die?

In Christianity, Jesus rose from the dead on the third day and ascended into Heaven, but not before promising that he would come again, the same way he left, in the clouds. Only this time, every eye would see him... including those that pierced him. Because of Jesus' sacrifice, suffering, and embodiment of all things good, we hope for an eternal life of pure bliss in Heaven. If we do not accept this sacrifice and become born again, we will suffer torture and agony in hell.

Our questions are answered. Yes, there is suffering and pain, but it's because we deserve it, and thanks to Jesus, we will soon see an end to all the suffering. We will soon find ourselves where all nations will exist under one law, theirs, and there will be no divergence from that law. This is also comforting in the face of mankind's greatest challenge, the environmental crises we now face. Fundamentalists resist Climate Change because they believe God gave them dominion over the Earth; therefore, it's their right to do with the Earth as they please. Ultimately, Jesus is coming back, so they will be safe from any repercussions of their actions to the Earth.

So, how do we protect ourselves and our Earth from these beliefs?

That's the biggest challenge we face. We can't fight these beliefs with reason because they're fear-based. This isn't a logical debate; it's an emotional debate, but their stronghold is crumbling. The Universe itself is dismantling its arguments rather quickly. Most scientists have given up arguing the science of evolution since the science is indisputable. Yet the Fundamentalist's fear won't acknowledge it. So, as long as they can, Creationists will struggle to produce "facts" that will support their dogma.

This debate is volatile because of the way beliefs work. When beliefs are challenged, those who adhere to them become terrified and lash out like caged animals. We've been watching it for some time now, and the higher the scientific evidence piles up, the crazier the Fundamentalists are becoming. Those who adhere to this belief system will kill to protect that system. Still, God is God regardless of how things started, and when we set God free, we're free.

It is this system of beliefs that keeps the anti-gay industry alive. It's Adam and Eve, the Garden of Eden, the serpent—without those, there is no reason for the anti-gay movement to exist. Without the Garden of Eden, there would be no template for human sexuality. There would be no "sin" and no "morality." Humanity would recognize that how we treat each other is a man-made construct.

Another challenge to the Adam and Eve objection is the two creation stories themselves.

In Genesis 1:3—2:4, the first story of creation, God (Elohim), creates the Earth, animals, and humankind. Very little fanfare is made over the creation of humankind. There's no separation between them. Genesis 1:26-27 puts it very succinctly: "Then God (Elohim) said, 'Let us make man in our image, in our likeness, and let them rule over the fish of the sea and the birds of the air, over the livestock, over all the earth, and over all the creatures that move along the ground.' So God created man in his image, in the image of God he created him; male and female he created them."

This brings up some interesting questions.

First, who is "us" in this story? Who was God talking to, and what did he mean by "image" since God doesn't have an image? This is an important question as it will say as much about God as it does about us.

The second question is, "Who is man?" The verse says, "God created man in his image," and then, "Male and female he created them." The author doesn't tell us if both Adam and Eve were created in the image of God or if Adam was in the image of God and Eve was in the image of Adam. Is the author of the first creation story (E) saying that man and women were created at the same time and both in the image of God? Or is it making the case that Adam was male and female starting out and then somehow separated by God? How did God create the female in this story, and what was the timeline?

If God created Adam and Eve (men and women) in his image simultaneously, then is God a hermaphrodite so that both men and women looked like him in one way or another? The first author is nondescript.

This is significant because, with all these questions about the nature of the first humans, there's enough uncertainty that it doesn't make the cut-and-dry argument that Fundamentalists think it does.

In the second creation story, Genesis 2:4—25, God (YHWH) forms Adam before anything else. "And no shrub of the field had yet appeared on the earth, and no plant of the field had yet sprung up, for the LORD God had not sent rain on the earth and there was no man to work the ground, but streams came up from the earth and watered the whole surface of the ground- the LORD God formed the man from the dust of the ground and breathed into his nostrils the breath of life, and the man became a living being."

YHWH then creates a garden (Eden) for Adam to live in. He places two trees in the middle of the garden: The Tree of Life and the Tree of the Knowledge of Good and Evil.

Almost immediately after Adam is in the garden, YHWH starts to rethink his creation. In the first story of creation, Elohim ended every creative session (each day) with the phrase, "and God (Elohim) saw that it was good." That is not how YHWH felt after creating Adam. The first thing out of his mouth was: "The LORD God said, 'It is not good for the man to be alone. I will make a helper suitable for him.'"

With Adam in the garden and the foliage created, YHWH concludes that Adam needs a helper or help-mate. So, to come up with the perfect helper, he goes on to form all the animals. Once he's finished, he brings them to Adam individually for Adam to name. When Adam is done naming the animals, YHWH determines that none of them are suitable as a helpmate for Adam. That's when he puts Adam to sleep, pulls out one of his ribs, and creates a counterpart, which Adam names "Woman."

No sooner did YHWH create Eve when she found herself hanging out near the Tree of the Knowledge of Good and Evil and met a serpent. The serpent advises her to go ahead and eat the fruit, which she does and then takes some to Adam.

One of the many ironies of this story is what the food represented... knowledge. What could be wrong with knowledge?

The biggest irony, though, was their state of dress. Their eyes were open, and they saw that they were naked. Was it a sin to be naked? If so, why did God create them naked? Is it only a sin to be naked if you know you're naked? They saw themselves as they were, in their purest state, in their 'innocence,' and were ashamed.

However, the second creation story makes it very clear that God didn't have any particular "helpmate" in mind and that Eve was an afterthought. Therefore, it wasn't ever in the mind of God that it would be man and woman. It was in the mind of God that man needed a helpmate. In that context, homosexuality fits in just fine since we still fulfill the purpose.

The Fundamentalist's favorite narrative is the perceived "Wrath of God" on Homosexuality based on the Stories of Sodom and Gomorrah. Most Fundamentalists know this story well, and they quote it with delight. They get almost orgasmic as they tell it. For the sake of those who aren't familiar with this oft-told vengeful tale, I'll briefly recap so you'll have the basics.

I guess the first thing I should do here is introduce you to the cast of characters. God is at the top in a starring role, and His costar is Abraham. In this story, we don't see much of either, but they played a vital role in the fate of Sodom and Gomorrah. Then there's Abraham's nephew, Lot, one of the residents of Sodom. Lot had a wife and two daughters (both virgins, as you will soon find out). Rounding off the cast are two angels. The setting occurs in the plains just north of the Dead Sea, surrounded by cliffs and rocks.

In this infamous story, God decided that he had had about as much as he could take from "The Cities of the Plain," which Sodom and Gomorrah were the two most famous. "The stench of their sins" had reached him all the way into heaven, which is what he told Abraham one day during a visit. That must have been some stench since it would take thousands of years traveling at the speed of light to get out of our galaxy, let alone to heaven. So Abraham pleaded with God not to destroy the cities if he found any righteous people living there, and God promised that he wouldn't as long as that provision was met.

Genesis 19 opens with two angels walking into Sodom. Abraham's nephew, Lot, sits at the gate when he sees them. There's no reason given for the angels' visit. Were they there to find the alleged "righteous" citizens of Sodom? Were they on reconnaissance? Maybe they were there to warn Lot. The truth is, we're not told. We don't know what Lot was doing at the city gate either. Who sits at the gate of a city? Was he begging? Was he on the welcoming committee? Was he on the lookout for strangers? Was he changing the locks?

Lot sees the two angels and takes them to his house, fearing for their safety, but they don't get there unseen. That night, all the men of the city show up at Lot's house demanding the two angels so that they may "know" (i.e., have sex with) them. Lot is appalled by their actions, so to save them, he offers in their place his two daughters, who had "never known a man" (or had never had sex with a man). In other words, they were virgins.

This act only made the men angrier, and they threatened Lot with the same treatment. Just as the men reach Lot's front door, one of the angels pulls Lot back inside, and the men of Sodom are struck with blindness. They then tell Lot to take his family and get out of town that night before God rained down fire on them. He and his family were also warned not to look back.

Lot was rather attached to Sodom, so the angels literally took him by the hand and led him out of the city, telling him and his family to head for the hills. Lot protested and asked if he could head to a small nearby city. "It's a small city," he told the angels, so they agreed, but he had to hurry. So, for Lot's sake, they spared the city of Zoar.

Lot took his wife and two daughters, leaving Sodom just before dawn. As the angels promised, as Lot's family left the city, fire came down from Heaven. Lot's wife looked back and turned into a pillar of salt, thus proving throughout history that God hates fags and the women who look back upon them (i.e., fag-hags). But it turns out that

Lot was still afraid and left Zoar and headed for the hills anyway, where he dwelt in a cave with his daughters.

What amazes me most about this story is that nobody seems bothered that God would take it upon himself to come to a city to destroy men, women, and children—allegedly his children. Isn't that out of character for a God of love? Is that how a loving father behaves toward any of his children? What about these "men of Sodom?" Even in San Francisco, where vast amounts of men are gay, you would still be hard-pressed to find a situation where "every man in the city" would come out and demand to know two strangers.

There are several other troubling events that nobody seems to care to discuss either. In my mind, the most troubling thought is this—Lot is considered a righteous man—even though he was willing to give up his two daughters to be raped by a mob of angry men to protect two people he didn't even know. The men of Sodom were considered evil because they wanted to have sex with two angels (adults) but were unwilling to rape two innocent girls, probably eleven or twelve, since they hadn't been with a man, which usually happened at the age of thirteen or fourteen). Does that sound backward? Granted, rape is unwelcome, but let's ask, "What kind of father would throw his daughters to a mob of men like that, specifically emphasizing their virginity?"

Now Lot is a widower, and his only companions are the two daughters he was ready to sacrifice a few hours ago. While living in their cave, the two daughters decide they don't want to die virgins, so they conspire to have children with the only man they know. They get their father drunk, and the oldest daughter sleeps with him. They get their father drunk again the next night, and the youngest daughter sleeps with him. Both girls get pregnant, and according to Genesis 19, their father has no recollection of what happened, even though it happened twice.

This raises some interesting questions, which I won't address here, but that's a lot of alcohol. I've been pretty drunk before, but I'm sure I would know if I committed incest (which wasn't officially banned until later in the book of Leviticus.). Second, for a man with that amount of alcohol in his system, there will be some performance issues. You see, the drunker the man gets, the less likely his equipment will work, right up to the point where he passes out.

Yet Lot's oldest daughter gave birth to a son named Moab. The youngest daughter gave birth to a son named Benammi, a.k.a. Ammon. And if you know anything about the history of Israel, these two groups of people made things difficult for the Tribes of Israel throughout most of their developmental years.

The God in this story doesn't sound like the father in the parable of the Prodigal Son. What further amazes me is that it seems that it's homosexuality, not rape or incest, that God finds repugnant.

Genesis 19 strikes me not as much as a condemnation of homosexuality but as a stark reminder that God's family is far more dysfunctional than those who oppose it. Yet these are the family values that Exodus International, Focus on the Family, and the other Ex-Gay ministries are trying to achieve.

If you look at the reasons for this horrific event, there aren't any. God tells Abraham that the stench of their sins has reached him, but what was that stench? Did it smell like homosexuality? Did it smell like soiled condoms? Did it smell like lube? Did it smell like the gym? We're not told, but throughout the Bible, Sodom and Gomorrah have been used to represent sins other than sexual. Usually, when you hear them mentioned, Sodom and Gomorrah are synonymous with greed and selfishness, not homosexuality. The only overt reference to the sins of Sodom and Gomorrah is in Ezekiel 16, where God accuses them of being greedy and selfish. He also claims they didn't help the poor, needy, widows, and orphans. And then he (God) accuses Israel of being worse than Sodom and Gomorrah.

There's also another option, though. It's been considered by scholars, and it does have some credence in the realm of Old Testament scholarship. Scholars have noted some interesting particulars about the story, starting with the word "know."

Most of us laypeople think that the word "know," as it's used in the Bible, refers to some sexual connection, as in, "And Adam knew Eve, his wife; and she conceived, and bare Cain, and said, I have gotten a man from the Lord." However, only in the King James version of the Bible is the word know used in this context.

The Hebrew verb "to know" occurs 943 times in the Old Testament. Of those 943 occurrences, only ten refer to "carnal knowledge," such as Genesis 4:1. Genesis 19:5 would be the only place in the Bible where "know" refers to homosexual relations. So, out of the 943 occurrences, 933 of those times, the verb "know" means "know." Nine out of the 943 times, "know" means carnal knowledge between a man and a woman. One time out of the 943 times, "know" means gay carnal knowledge.

Within that context, it would mean that Lot (who was not himself a citizen of Sodom but still a sojourner) invited two people to his home at night, though he did not have the authority to do so. So, the men of the city showed up and demanded that Lot bring out the men he was hiding so that they might "know them." In other words, they wanted to interrogate the strangers and find out what they were doing there in the first place. The outcome could have been tragic for Lot's guests as they could have been put out of the city or killed. Because the city elders did not invite them, they were considered a threat.

This might also make more sense from Lot's counteroffer to the mob in offering his virgin daughters to appease them. It makes sense that if the men were straight, they would be more tempted to take Lot up on his offer. If the men had come to rape two men, why would Lot consider that they might be tempted by his two daughters instead?

The result of this translation would lead to the conclusion that the cities of the plain, Sodom and Gomorrah, were destroyed for the sin of inhospitality: "Behold, this was the iniquity of thy sister Sodom, pride, fullness of bread, and abundance of idleness was in her and her daughters, neither did she strengthen the hand of the poor and needy. And they were haughty and committed abomination before me: therefore, I took them away as I saw good."

(Ezekiel 16:49)

Jesus himself may have believed this to be the case when he gave this command to his disciples: "Whosoever shall not receive you, nor hear your words, when you depart out of that house or city, shake off the dust of our feet. Verily I say unto you, it shall be more tolerable for the land of Sodom and Gomorrah in the day of judgment than for that city."

(Matthew 10:14-15, Luke 10:10-12)

Another thing that frightens Christians is the perceived attack on "Family Values," specifically, "Biblical Family Values" that homosexuality represents. I remember receiving an e-mail at work from a friend. It seemed a certain domestic brewery was planning to use a homosexual couple in one of their beer advertisements. In my friend's "concern," she sent an e-mail to everyone on her e-mail list asking them to write or call the company, protest the advertisement, and threaten to boycott it altogether. Of course, I was still hiding in my closet then, so she sent it to me, thinking I felt the same way she did. In jest, I sent back an e-mail asking her if she knew the number to support the ad. She responded by reminding me that "I couldn't be serious," which upset me. So I sent back another e-mail to this effect.

First, I asked, are Christians supposed to frequent establishments like this? Her response to that was that she had a problem with the ad. She didn't want her children and her nieces and nephews growing up under the influence of this "abomination." Now I was really upset. Friend or not, I was not going to be silent about that.

What I've noticed about Christianity is that they're looking for utopia. Some place where they can live in peace and harmony. Some place where everyone thinks and acts as they do. Some place where there's no freedom of choice or expression. Everybody's always doing the same thing, and nobody's offending them. It sounds like an excellent world, but it isn't the world I live in, and when we try to create such a place, we end up with a little thing called the Inquisition or the Salem Witch Trials.

I remember watching the news one day after the Bill Clinton and Monica Lewinsky story broke. They were interviewing protesters, and I saw one self-righteous man reach into his wallet, pull out a picture of his kids, and show it to the reporter. "What am I going to tell my kids?" he asked. At the time, I thought, "Tell them the truth" as carefully as possible to a child, and then help them understand how much trouble the president is in and why." This was the perfect opportunity to teach the children about actions and consequences.

Of course, history has revealed that the Bill Clinton affair had nothing to do with sex. It was politically motivated.

This brings up another thought: Christians hate sex. Of all the world's evils, sex is right up there at the top. You look at any protest, rant, or condemnation, and sex is at the heart of it. Some unsanctioned sexual involvement defines every definition of immorality.

As a gay man, being "responsible" for everybody else's kids is frustrating. They don't want me to be gay because they don't want their kids to grow up in an environment where gay people are given a voice. They don't want me speaking my mind because their kids might hear me and soften their views toward me, and that would bring them mental distress and challenge their perfect utopian beliefs.

I agree that children are impressionable and that they should be offered as much protection as we can healthily give them, but to shelter them from the world around them does them a great disservice since, sooner or later, they're going to have to grow up and live in this big evil world. Any person bringing children into the world does so at their own risk and shouldn't expect society to change the rules because of their choice to have a child.

They're using homosexuals in beer commercials (which I think is odd because most of us drink Cosmos or Appletinis). If you want to make the world a better place, teach the children about the world—it's got its ups and downs, and there are a whole plethora of people living in it. If we try to shelter children from the world, they may become like us: unable to deal with diversity and striving desperately to make everyone around them conform rather than learning how to live with their neighbors. Isn't this what causes wars? Six billion people are a lot of people to try and change, but one person, the person you see when you look into the mirror every morning, that's much easier.

Let's address this Biblical Family Values issue by looking at some of the most remarkable men of the Bible and their families, starting with Adam and Eve and their sons Cain and Abel. It's a familiar story, but again, here's the basic storyline from Genesis 4 for those unfamiliar.

The older brother Cain was a farmer, or as the Bible says, "tilled the soil," and Abel, the younger brother, was a shepherd. He "kept the flocks." Both appeared before God to offer up a sacrifice. "Cain brought some of the fruits of the soil as an offering to the Lord." And Abel brought "fat portions from some of the firstborn of his livestock." The Lord looked favorably on Abel's offering, but for some reason, he didn't look so favorably on Cain's. We're never told why, but it made Cain jealous. There is a conversation where God tells Cain that if he does what is right, then God will look favorably on his sacrifice, but again, we're never explicitly told what God is looking for (isn't that always the way with God). What is it that Cain needs to do to get on God's good side?

So, Cain set up a meeting with his brother somewhere in a field, and when Abel showed up, "Cain attacked his brother, Abel, and killed him."

Then God asked Cain, "Where is your brother Abel?"

Cain replied, "I don't know. Am I my brother's keeper?"

God knew where Abel was; of course, he was angry with Cain and cursed him so that when he worked the ground, it would no longer yield crops to him. He also told Cain he would be a restless wanderer on the earth. So the first thing Cain did was get a wife of his own (presumably one of his sisters), have kids, and build a city in the land of Nod (I guess he could have been restless: what with traffic and the noisy neighbors upstairs, and those damn kids and their music blaring at 120 decibels).

Abraham, the great patriarch and founder of Israel, always wanted a son. On many occasions, God promised Abraham that his children would be like the 'sands of the sea' or like 'the stars in the sky.' But at age eighty-six, Abraham was still childless. So Abraham's wife, Sarah, had a wild idea. She had an Egyptian servant named Hagar. She told Abraham to take Hagar as his wife and marry her.

As luck would have it, Hagar "conceived," as the Bible says. But things didn't go well between her and Sarah. She "began to despise her mistress." So Sarah went to Abraham again, and while this whole affair was her idea, she blamed Abraham.

"You are responsible for the wrong I am suffering," she told Abraham.

Abraham responded by saying, "Your servant is in your hands. Do with her whatever you think best."

So, Sarah mistreated Hagar, and Hagar fled. The Angel of the Lord found Hagar near a spring in the desert and told her to return and submit to her mistress. So, Hagar returned and bore Abraham's first son, Ishmael. However, Isaac, Abraham's second son and first son from his wife Sarah, got all the press and Abraham's blessings—not to mention his money.

As a reward for being God's favorite, God demands that Abraham take Isaac to the top of Mount Moriah and offer him up as a sacrifice.

Of course, God stepped in at the last minute, but imagine, if you will, your father tying you up, laying you on a bunch of kindling, preparing to drive a dagger through your heart, and then lighting you on fire.

We like to think of Jacob, the younger twin of Esau, son of Isaac, and grandson of Abraham, as one of the great patriarchs of the Bible, but Jacob was a cheat, a liar, and a thief. First, he used extortion to get his brother's birthright. His brother Esau, who was a hunter, came to him hungry. Jacob would only feed him in return for Esau's birthright as the older brother.

When it came time for Isaac to give his sons the final blessing before he died (which included the inheritance and all his possessions), his mother concocted a scheme. "When Isaac was old, and his eyes were so weak that he could no longer see, he called for Esau, his older son." Sensing that Isaac was about to give Esau the blessing, Rebekah, Jacob's mom, dressed her younger son to look, smell, and feel like Esau. Thus, Jacob again got the blessing to go to Esau. But his deception doesn't end there. The list of Jacob's deceptions covers several chapters of the book of Genesis. He was so bad that God had to eventually change his name before he could carry on his lineage of the father of Israel.

Aaron, the brother of Moses also the first high priest of Israel in the Sinai desert, had two sons, Nadab and Abihu. They also were ordained as priests by God and by Moses. Then they decided to disrespect the temple for some reason, and "they took their censers, put fire in them and added incense, and offered unauthorized fire before the Lord, contrary to his command."

If there's one thing you'll learn quickly as you read through the Bible, "Don't piss God off." Well, Nadab and Abihu did just that. So fire came from the presence of the Lord and consumed them, and Aaron was told that he wasn't to mourn his two sons.

The book of Judges has another fine example of Biblical Family Values. In Judges 11, a man named Jephthah was locked in a battle with the Ammonites (remember Ammon, the grandson of Lot?). In a desperate attempt to win the battle against the Ammonites, Jephthah promised God, "If you give the Ammonites into my hands, whatever comes out of the door of my house to meet me when I return in triumph from the Ammonites will be the Lord's, and I will sacrifice it as a burnt offering." Well, shucks, wouldn't you know it? The first person out the door was his daughter and only child, dancing to the sound of tambourines.

When Jephthah saw his daughter, he tore his clothes and told her of his vow to the Lord. All in all, she was pretty understanding. "My father," she replied. "You have given your word to the Lord. Do to me just as you promised." But then she makes one more request. It's an odd request, but it makes sense. "Give me two months to roam the hills and weep with my friends because I will never marry."

So, she went away and wept over her virginity for two months and then returned. I would have gotten out of there, but she didn't. Instead, she returned home, and her father "did to her as he vowed."

Another tragic part of this story is that Jephthah probably wouldn't have cared if it had been anyone else. If it were one of his servants, he would have dispatched them quickly without even allowing them a last request. This represents the mindset of the Fundamentalists. They only care about their own. The only family values they care about are their families. If it's not their family, they don't care.

The stories of David and his family are epic tales of family dysfunction.

One night, David is walking on the roof of his castle and sees Bathsheba taking a bath on her roof. So he invites her over. She informs David that she's married. Her husband, Uriah the Hittite, is a soldier in David's army fighting for his king, but David sleeps with her anyway.

Soon, she reveals to her king that she's pregnant, so David has Uriah brought home for some special time with his wife so that he will be off the hook. But Uriah is loyal to his king and does not sleep with his wife. Instead, he sleeps at the palace entrance with David's servants. So David tries another approach—this time, he sends Uriah to the battlefront with a letter to his general, Joab. Uriah isn't privy to the information in this letter (although he delivered it) or may have been more reluctant to pass it on. In this letter, David told Joab to put Uriah on the front lines of battle, and as soon as it got heated, Joab and his men were to pull back, and Uriah would be left alone.

So that's exactly what happened. Uriah was dead, betrayed by his king, and David was scandal-free.

Later in the story, David's son Amnon falls in love with his sister Tamar. "He became frustrated to the point of illness" because he couldn't do anything to her. So he set up a little scheme. He had his friend, Jonadab, tell Tamar that Amnon was ill so she could minister to him. It worked. Amnon pretended to be sick, and David sent Tamar to care for him. When she arrived, Amnon raped her, but once he had his jollies, "he hated her. He hated her with intense hatred. He hated her more than he had loved her."

He told her to get out.

She told him that making her leave would be an even greater crime than the rape, but they threw her out and bolted the door behind her. She could no longer wear the robes of a virgin because of her attack, and she could no longer marry either because of the customs in Israel.

Tamar was Absalom's favorite sister. He loved her deeply, and when he heard this, he was understandably angry, setting the scene for his attempted coup d'état several years later.

Absalom did have his revenge. He took his brother to a celebration at Baal Hazor. When his brother was in high spirits from excess wine, Absalom's servants slew him as Absalom instructed them. And yet Absalom is portrayed as the bad guy.

Ironically, the one king with a good child was Saul, the father of Jonathan—of David and Jonathan. Jonathan was faithful to David, true to God, and true to Israel. He was everything God said he wanted in a king, yet God took the kingdom from Jonathan and handed it over to David, who wasn't true to anyone but himself.

Go figure.

It's also worth noting that David never met a woman he didn't marry. Between him and his son Solomon, they probably married half the known female population at that time. It was common for men to have many wives back then, and women were just property.

These are just some of the stories in the Bible. These are the family values that Focus on the Family is afraid that homosexuality is threatening. I don't care how great the Bible says these men were; I do not share their family values. Christianity talks at great lengths about love, but this is not love, and Jesus didn't change that. He said he "came to turn mother against daughter and father against son." When approached by his family, he publicly disowned them, claiming that only those who listened to him were his family.

The family values of the Bible do not constitute family or even values. As I've read through these stories, the one thing I've noticed missing throughout them is "values." These highly dysfunctional people should not be emulated but should instead serve as a stark reminder of how important it is that we develop spiritually so that we no longer propagate these behaviors.

What threatens Biblical Family Values is not homosexuality, television, rock and roll, not Democrats, not even pornography, or a president getting a hummer in the Oval Office. What threatens Biblical Family Values is the Bible itself. As humans become more "civilized," these behaviors are no longer acceptable to us. We are learning that we should no longer tolerate violence against children. We are learning that it is deplorable to tolerate the subjugation of women or the proliferation of slavery. We are learning that families must act responsibly toward one another and the communities around them if humans can survive. Even in God's name, we are learning to find these things appalling and unacceptable. These Biblical events may have been acceptable when survival was much more difficult, but it is no longer acceptable, and that's why Biblical Family Values are under attack. Society is now looking for a place where children are loved and cherished, all children are cared for, fed, and nurtured, and we're less concerned about what that family has to look like.

I knew a lot of Christians growing up, and there's one thing I can tell you. Most of their upbringing wasn't good. If you look at the basic structure of most churches, you will see that they're set up to subjugate children, suppress women, and control their members. This is where today's society is finally starting to break free. I believe that if every child on this planet were to know they were loved and cherished (not that homosexuality was wrong), then we would have heaven on earth.

I once watched a television talk show where the topic was gay adoption. All through the show, one man kept protesting that if they allowed gay adoptions, then the kids would turn out gay. My first thought about this argument was that every gay and lesbian person I had ever met was the product of "straight" parents, not gay parents. My parents were both straight. Sexuality is in the hard drive, not the software. I can't share my gay hardware with anyone, no matter how much I wish I could. And believe me, I had a lot of friends who would have been perfect candidates for any file-sharing software, were that possible.

I'd also like to use a little bit of math. For some reason, people compare sexuality (hard drive) to environment (software) and sex (behavior). I can understand because it looks so similar. So, this is where the math comes in. Let's say I have an equation. It looks like this: $X^3 + X^2 + X$, and I'm told to simplify that as far as I can. Can I simplify this any further? The answer is no. While X^3 and X^2 and X may look similar, they are three completely different integers. That is the best way to try and explain the differences between sexuality, environment, and upbringing. They're very different.

Another thing that bothered me about this man's argument was that in his obsession with averting any further homosexuality, he lost sight of something that I think is even more important. Most kids up for adoption wouldn't have a family life otherwise. Even though there are people who want to take these kids and give them a chance at a happy life, this man would rather that these kids stay in their troubled lives rather than find the support of someone who loves them just because he doesn't care for their disparity from his own viewpoint. That, to me, is the biggest tragedy. It reveals that Fundamentalists are not Pro-Life. Life is about diversity, love, and making sure that all those in need are supported and loved. Fundamentalists are just anti-abortion. That's completely different.

Then, of course, there are the infamous four verses in the Bible that ban homosexuality. They are in their entirety so that you can see them for yourself.

The first one appears in a list of sexual prohibitions in the book of Leviticus.

> "Do not lie with a man as one lies with a woman, that is detestable.
> *Leviticus 18:22*

> If a man lies with a man as one lies with a woman, both have done what is detestable. They must be put to death; their blood will be on their own heads.

> *Leviticus 20:13*

> Therefore, God gave them over in the sinful desires of their hearts to sexual impurity for the degrading of their bodies with one another.

They exchanged the truth of God for a lie and worshiped and served created things rather than the Creator—who is forever praised. Amen.

Because of this, God gave them over to shameful lusts. Even their women exchanged natural relations for unnatural ones.

In the same way, the men also abandoned natural relations with women and were inflamed with lust for one another. Men committed indecent acts with other men and received in themselves the due penalty for their perversion.

Romans 1:24-27.

Do you not know that the wicked will not inherit the kingdom of God? Do not be deceived: Neither the sexually immoral nor idolaters nor adulterers nor male prostitutes nor homosexual offenders...

1 Corinthians 6:9

And that is what some of you were.
1 Corinthians 6:11

Well, there you have it. That seems cut-and-dry. You can't argue with those injunctions, can you? But let's look at what else Paul said in Corinthians, just a few verses later.

Now for the matters you wrote about. It is good for a man not to marry. But since there is so much immorality, each man should have his own wife and each woman her own husband.

1 Corinthians 1:1-2

Christians love to use this verse as a ban on Gay marriages, saying that true marriage is a union of one man and one woman, but Paul is just making marriage a concession to those who can't handle their morality.

> I say this as a concession, not as a command.
> *1 Corinthians 7:6*

> But if they cannot control themselves, they should marry, for it is better to marry than to burn with passion.
>
> *1 Corinthians 7:9*

Paul also has some other commands alongside the ban on homosexuality, and I don't see these rules enforced anymore.

> Every man who prays or prophesies with his head covered dishonors his head. And every woman who prays or prophesies with her head uncovered dishonors the head—it is just as though her head were shaved. If a woman does not cover her head, she should have her hair cut off, and if it is a disgrace for a woman to have her hair cut or shaved off, she should cover her head.

1 Corinthians 11:4-6

> Judge for yourselves: Is it proper for a woman to pray to God with her head uncovered? Does not the very nature of things teach you that if a man has long hair, it is a disgrace to him, but that if a woman has long hair, it is her glory? For long hair is given to her as a covering. If anyone wants to be contentious about this, we have no other practice—nor do the churches of God.

1 Corinthians 11:15

In Leviticus, an injunction says, "Do not come near a woman during her period of uncleanness to uncover her nakedness." Leviticus 18:19. I don't hear that one preached from the pulpit too often. In Leviticus 20:18, the same injunction is repeated a little differently. "If a man lies with a woman in her infirmity and uncovers her nakedness, he has laid bare her flow, and she has exposed her blood flow; both shall be cut off from among their people."

In Leviticus 20:8 it reads, "You shall faithfully observe my laws. I, the Lord, make you holy."

Let's look at that closely. According to this passage, God's laws are to be obeyed. There isn't anything in this scripture that says "some of my laws." Jesus even went so far as to say if you break one commandment, you've broken them all. In the Pentateuch, there are over six hundred laws, and if we want to take one out of there, we must take them all out. That means you can't show deference to the rich. You can't sow two types of seed in the same field. You can't eat blood if you eat meat. There are several types of meat you can't eat. There were many laws about sacrificial lambs, scapegoats, holidays, religious ceremonies, and cleanliness. You can't lift one of the scriptures from this passage unless you're prepared to use them all. This is true of Leviticus and Corinthians.

In my copy of the Torah, translated from Hebrew by the Jewish Publication Society, they have this to say about this verse.

Far more controversial, from the modern standpoint, is the outright condemnation of sexual relations between males—conduct for which the death penalty is prescribed. We have no record of a death sentence for this crime being carried out under Jewish auspices....

In his famous 1935 letter to the concerned mother of a homosexual man, Sigmund Freud wrote, "Homosexuality is assuredly no advantage, but it is nothing to be ashamed of, no vice, no degradation, it cannot be classified as an illness."

...

In many cultures, there has been little or no objection to homosexual behavior. The ancient Egyptians condemned it, but it was widespread among the Greeks. In the Athens of Pericles and Plato, love affairs between teenage boys and older men were frequent. They were even considered beneficial for the intellectual and moral development of the younger party. Even in societies that officially ban such practices, they occur more frequently than former generations supposed—or at least admitted. Homosexual behavior has also been noted among lower animals as well...

Our greatest needs at present are to gain more knowledge on the subject—knowledge sought objectively—and to ensure that individual reactions to this admittedly sensitive subject do not deny the simple justice and fairness of homosexual women and men.

The Torah—A Modern Commentary pp881-883

Edited by W. Gunther Plaut

Published by the Jewish Publication Society

But it can be argued that the command was reaffirmed in the New Testament, which makes it credible, right?

What makes me crazy about those who use the Bible to condemn homosexuality is that so many are fat. Nothing is more insulting than Fat Fundies screaming that homosexuals are degrading their bodies.

The Bible has just as much to say about gluttony as any other sin, yet gluttony is rampant in the church, and it's completely ignored. Obesity and the diseases that accompany it are so prevalent that the church has just now decided that they need to talk about it.

Many fundamentalists will say, "Sin is sin in the eyes of God," and completely overlook their sin as they sit down to a Denny's Grand Slam breakfast with extra bacon, eggs over easy, salt for the hash browns and lots of syrup for those pancakes. And while you're eating, don't forget to insult your wait staff for not getting your order right and then stiff them on the tip.

> Do you not know that your body is a temple of the Holy Spirit, who is in you, whom you have received from God? You are not your own;
>
> You were bought at a price. Therefore, honor God with your body.

I Corinthians 6:19-20

> Be not among drunkards or among gluttonous eaters of meat, for the drunkard and the glutton will come to poverty, and slumber will clothe them with rags.

Proverbs 23:20-21

> Remove far from me falsehood and lying; give me neither poverty nor riches; feed me with the food that is needful for me,

Proverbs 30:8

> Be not among drunkards or among gluttonous eaters of meat,

Proverbs 23:20

And put a knife to your throat if you are given to appetite.

Proverbs 23:2

When I talk about my experiences, someone will often approach me and say, "But I know someone who's changed." I even sometimes talk to those who tell me they have succeeded. If I pursue the issue with them, I know there will be several caveats to their change. First, they must avoid any place where temptation will be available. Second, they have to avoid any contact with any homosexual who is being themselves for fear they'll be led astray themselves. Finally, they can never talk about homosexuality being good under any circumstances. They have to blame their past problems on their sexuality.

I've never met anyone who, I believe, has changed, and even if they did, I know many more who have abandoned any semblance of spirituality simply because they couldn't beat this thing. God wasn't at all interested in helping them.

So again, let's look at the hard drive and the spectrum of sexuality.
The Gay Scale

|||

Gay Bi Straight

Depending on where you are on this line, I think, has a lot to do with how successful you're going to be at any attempt to change. Those in the middle of the Gay/Straight line can focus their attention on one side or the other and live there comfortably for quite some time. They would be what we call bi-sexual.

Others find that they would like to experiment and see what it's like on the other side, but that's because they're a little further away from "straight" on the scales. Then there are also those of us on the "gay" side of this spectrum. I've seen interviews with those who have claimed they have changed (there aren't very many, but there are a few), and most of the time, they look to me as if they're not telling the truth about their true feelings and instead are trying to force themselves to the other side of this line. This is borne out by the plethora of reports of those who thought they had changed and then suddenly uprooted their families and tore their lives apart because they couldn't "continue to live a lie." It's the beach ball syndrome all over again. Only this time, unfortunately, there were other people involved.

I read a book early on in my Ex-Gay expedition called "Beyond Rejection," and the man who wrote it claimed to be raped by his stepfather. As a result, he, too, found himself gay. The truth is, though, I don't think that's how it worked. What I hear most often about child abuse and molestation is that the child perpetuates the abuse continually in their development as they grow and mature. That means if a same-sex parent or adult raped a child, the child may perpetuate that abuse for many years, trying to deal with all the emotions present during the experience. As the abused adult seeks help and works through those issues, their true sexuality will be restored. Notice what I said here. Their true sexuality will be restored.

The molestation argument is a favorite of Ex-Gay counselors, and most will try to convince their clients that their homosexuality started with inappropriate contact with men in authority. I heard that as well.

When I heard this the first time, I was shocked. Granted, I didn't remember much about my childhood, but it seemed that something like that would stand out. So the first time I heard it, I rejected it because I couldn't remember anything. However, when something is repeated enough, you consider it might be true. So, eventually, I started to consider it. I figured it had to be one of my mom's boyfriends. I knew it couldn't have been my father since that man wanted nothing to do with me, and I knew it couldn't have been Roger since I was already feeling those feelings before he showed up; I just wasn't aware of them yet.

After her divorce and before she met Roger, my mom dated. Of course, she did. I don't think it was an excessive amount of men; I only remember a few. Some of her dates even spent the night. A couple of them were there often because they were more serious. So, I started looking for something in my past that might point to which of these men either molested me or touched me inappropriately.

After hours of Soul searching and a lot of sincere prayer, I had to conclude that there was no molestation. I told my counselor that I couldn't find anything in the back of my head to support his assertion and that I didn't think it was fair to make accusations that couldn't be supported. So, the issue was dropped, and we moved on to the next topic.

Every gay person I've ever talked to tells me the same thing. They all knew they were different by the age of ten and before. As I said earlier, it's not a choice but a discovery. As I go through this explanation with people, they respond—"But Mickey did it. He's successful. He's a father with two college-age boys. He leads an Ex-Gay group and helps others overcome their homosexuality. That means he's been successful for at least that long."

During our meetings, Mickey used to tell a story about something that happened between him and his mom. When his mom found out that he was gay, she stood in the middle of the room, tore up his picture, and pronounced to him that Mickey was no longer her son. Mickey cried and said, "I'll change Mama, I promise."

Mickey's mom has been dead for some time, but it was complicated based on what I've heard about their relationship. I think there's a lot more going on around that issue, and I wonder if Mickey has dealt with that, but by his admission, Mickey must avoid Seattle (especially the Capitol Hill Area), and he encourages others to do so. That would tell me that he's changed his behavior but hasn't changed his orientation.

It's also important to point out that I know of only two men in Mickey's group who claim to be successful. I know of at least thirty who have come and gone and are now living their "homosexual lives," as Mickey would call it. The success rate in Mickey's group is abysmal, and if any other organization claimed that kind of success, they would be dismantled. The Ex-Gay groups are the only groups I know of where the success of one or two persons is celebrated and used as a model for everyone else.

An old Buddhist saying is especially relevant here: "It works all the time, or it doesn't work." According to that observation, the Ex-Gay groups, including Mickey's, don't work.

Finally, the all-time classic is "It's the Mother/Father's fault." I once had a guy try and tell me that 'the reason I was gay was because of the relationship I had with my father.' Now, I've had many people tell me that, and at one time, that's what I believed, but my response to him made this one stand out. I started laughing. Then I asked him, "Do you know anyone... anyone at all... someone whose brother's sister's father-in-law's son's college roommate's best friend's little brother's stepdad's daughter's friend... who has had a good relationship with their

I was a Christian for nearly sixteen years, and in that time, I have seen just as many bad Christian fathers as I have ever seen outside the church. Quite frankly, inside the church, it's worse because the fathers can be abusive, and the children have to take it because they're Biblically obliged to submit to their parents. Absalom and Solomon had a rotten father, but they weren't gay. Isaac's father tried to kill him, but he wasn't gay. Cain's father was God's first son, and Cain didn't turn out well (at least according to legend).

Parenting plays a significant role in a child's upbringing, but let's face it: most of us have had some difficult times with our parents. Even if our parents tried to be good parents, they're only human, which means many mistakes were made. Even Jesus had issues with his parents. That's just the nature of growing up on planet Earth. Certain issues will get exaggerated, and specific problems that certain parenting styles can create, but that's like saying a lousy parent can make you shorter, taller, or of a different sex altogether.

LOOKING BACK

As I look back, I realize that I'm still not finished. I would love to talk about so much more that I haven't touched on. Instead, I'll restate what I said at the beginning. The God I discovered throughout my struggle emerged in a way I could have never expected or understood. This God looks so much different than the Christian God, but only because it can now be Itself without fitting into my image of how It should look. This God is much more powerful. This God is about love, and this God is about compassion because it comes from my identity, and therefore cares deeply about me. (I know that I've used the masculine for God during this article, but that's because I still tend to relate to God more in the masculine sense than the feminine, simply because "I'm in the masculine," and I love men.) I've never denied that I was deprived of a decent father, and I've never denied that the breakdown in that relationship hasn't caused problems, but I've learned over the years that even something that deep is very shallow when it comes to the Soul. Let me explain.

I like to use the metaphor of a child flying a kite. The child is small, and getting the kite into the wind is challenging. If the child's parent is there to help that child, the kite becomes more accessible because the parent has the height and know-how to lift the kite. Without the parent, the child may have a more challenging time. Either way, with practice, the kite will go into the air and fly once the child figures out how to use the wind. To some, that may seem rather simplistic as they believe I'm not dealing with the core issues of parent/child relationships. So, let me add one slight modification. We are that kite. Our parents are here to help and guide us so we may soar into the wind like the kite. Some of us didn't have the parental guidance we needed, and we had to struggle harder to get our kites—our Soul—into the air—but we did it. Once in the air, what happened on the ground is no longer relevant (provided we break the strings that tie us down and prevent us from soaring). That doesn't mean it didn't hurt. That doesn't detract from what happened, but even if you had the best parents in the world, you still have to get off the ground. Your parents can only get you so far. Conversely, they can only do so much to hold you down. The Soul was meant to fly, and every Soul wants to fly. So, any Soul that opens up even slightly finds itself discovering ways to hoist itself into the winds of change.

That's where forgiveness comes in. When I use the term forgiveness, I'm not talking about forgive and forget; I'm talking about something else. I look at forgiveness like this: when an event happens, it's like a ripple in the pond. It sends out waves rippling forward. An adverse event is set in motion, and the waves going forward are negative. So we do our forgiveness work, and the polarization of that event is then changed. The waves continue to go forward, but now they're changed. The events do not change, but the energy around them shifts. It's subtle, but it grows and expands, and as the energy is changed, we discover that a bad event can bring hope. Now, the original deed looks subtly different.

For instance, in my case, my father took away my right to defend myself. He used to laugh when other kids would beat me up, but he would never allow me to fight back. I grew up thinking that I wasn't worth defending. In the forgiveness work I did, several things happened.

First, I acknowledged everything I believed my father did to me that caused me pain. I didn't just acknowledge it; I got in touch with it. Then, I recognized that he didn't take anything from me. All that I needed was and still is there; I just needed to find a way to tap into it. This became clear in my relationship with God. I kept thinking that I needed someone outside of myself, and I got angry when God wouldn't fill that role.

Returning to my conversation about the levels of change and the Soul, my identity became that parent I needed to support me. My identity would stand up for me. My identity would teach me how to defend myself. My identity became what I needed in a father, and it did it far more thoroughly than my original father ever could.

Once I realized that my Identity was those things that I felt I needed from my father, I turned my need to judge this man over to God. While this wasn't exactly easy, it wasn't hard either. It mainly dealt with the part of me that wanted retribution for the sins committed against me.

I'm in the air now, though I don't know if I would say I'm soaring. I know there's a great height that I can attain, and I don't need that weight of unforgiveness holding me down. Like in Peter Pan, 'To fly you have to think happy thoughts,' the only way to get to those happy thoughts is to learn to forgive. That doesn't mean that the experiences of the past are meaningless; it just means that I gave them new meaning. Instead of accepting the label of victim, I turned this experience into something I could use to help rather than hold me back.

This experience means to me that I now have a mission. It's my turn to enter the fray. It's my turn to talk about what I've been through and why I could spend fifteen years trying to change and then realize it wasn't necessary. I want to talk to my fellow homosexuals and tell them they can be spiritual, find God, AND be gay. I want to talk to anyone who wants to understand this topic more and let them know that things aren't always what they seem. This is the new meaning I have put on my life and experience. That's what forgiveness has allowed me to do.

I have one last thing to say: I have been careful to differentiate between Christians and Fundamentalists. Christians believe their calling is to express the love and compassion that Jesus often spoke of. The Abba that Jesus loved so dearly was a father to all. They accept those who disagree with them, and they are the ones who would also say, "Father, forgive them, for they know not what they do."

On the other hand, Fundamentalists have taken a heavy-handed approach to the Bible. They value religion over spirituality. Some say, "I'm spiritual but not religious." On the other hand, Fundamentalists say, "I'm religious, but I'm not spiritual." The goal of the Fundamentalist is to create a one-world order where they are in control. They use politics as their weapon, and they recognize only their point of view. They view anyone who disagrees with them as an enemy to them and God.

This book is about Fundamentalists. Were it not for Fundamentalists, I don't think there would be a need to write this book. This is true of all the religions. The Jewish and Muslim religions all have their fundamentalists, but I know very little about their faith. I know that they are virulently anti-gay, but I don't think that there's anything in my story that would resonate with them. It would take others in their own religion to address them and their prejudice.

I hope that this issue won't be about Jesus, God, Allah, or YHWH someday soon, but that it will be about the human being who wants to be who they are without any fear of repercussion.

That's why this issue must be talked about. When a group of people believes they have the only way to God, they become dangerous, which I hope to prevent. There can be only one way to God for me, and that's my way. There can be only one way to God for you, and that's your way. In other words, there are as many ways to God as people on the planet.

If the Universe represents God, then we must assume that God is infinite. Based on simple physics, it would be impossible to limit those limitless options.

I want to leave with a little parable I wrote many years ago. Jesus liked to tell stories, which is the best way to communicate.

THE BLACK SHEEP

Last night, I had a dream and had to write it down when I woke up.

In this dream, I saw a birth. It was a baby lamb.

As the lamb entered the world, his parents, the Ewe and the Ram, looked lovingly upon him, doting incessantly. In my dream, they named him Lanny.

Lanny was a precious little life with only its mother and father to care for and clothe him.

As Lanny grew, he grew wool, and things started to go wrong for him.

The wool Lanny grew was black as night.

The little lamb looked at its reflection in the pond one day and noticed his wool was black and not white like his mother's and father's the rest of the flock.

Fear crept over him as he stared at his reflection, and I felt that terror in my dream, too. What was he to do?

He searched and found some cotton growing in a nearby field. He sauntered over to the field casually so that nobody would see him. Once there, he rolled in the cotton to cover every part of his skin so nobody could see the black wool.

The thorns and sticks from the cotton cut into his skin and hurt terribly, but he was safe from the ridicule of the rest of the flock.

This went on for a very long time; he could cover himself with cotton and protect his identity.

Nobody noticed.

Then, one day, the sheerer came to visit the flock. He rounded up the sheep and sheered their excess wool one by one.

Lanny watched in horror and tried to hide, but it was useless. The sheerer took his sheers and clipped the cotton away, exposing Lanny's secret.

Lanny was ashamed.

The rest of the flock stared at him in disbelief.

"How could this happen?" the Ram asked. "My family and I are upstanding members of this flock. I am a white sheep. I have white wool. My wife has white wool. All my other lambs have white wool."

Lanny hung his head in shame. "I'm sorry, father," he said. "I tried to cover it up." He looked at the rest of the flock. "I've done everything I could to be like you," he said, "but my wool keeps coming back black."

"Black wool is not right," one of the ewes whispered in a snit.

"Black wool is a sign of a perversion," another ram snorted. "You're wearing black wool; you're a freak of nature!"

"Maybe it's an abnormality?" another sheep questioned.

Soon, this little lamb would be brought before the council. At the head of the council was an old ram that had been in the flock for many years. He was considered wise and well-respected by the flock.

He looked the little lamb over carefully.

"I've seen such a thing before," he said. "For some reason, nature adds a little spice to the poor creature, and he stands out. Unfortunately, she does not consider how the poor creature will suffer due to his difference."

He looked back at the crowd. "I suggest he's just fine. Let him be. Accept him as your son and your brother and fellow flock member."

The sheep bleated and turned their backs on the elder. They would do no such thing. This was a black sheep, and he had no place in their society.

While discussing what to do with the poor little lamb, another ram who considered himself wise approached them.

"I have seen such things, too," he said. "And unlike my foolish colleague, I have a solution. I have a friend who has worked with lambs like yours, and he has found a solution."

So they sent the little lamb to this particular flock, which called themselves the "Recovering White Wool" flock. In this flock were many other lambs and sheep like himself who had once had black wool.

But now they had white wool. Their wool was so white that Lanny wondered if they were sheep at all.

The flock leader, Jefferson, got up and introduced Lanny to the rest of the group. Then he explained—"Having black wool is against nature, and therefore we must change it. If we allow ourselves to continue with our black wool, we will eventually be cut from the flock and not allowed access to the good shepherd."

Jefferson took Lanny and lay him down in the field as soon as he was done talking. Then he mixed a special dye. The dye stank and made Lanny's eyes water. Lanny's skin burned when they put the dye on his wool, and his nose swelled up. He could hardly breathe.

Jefferson looked him over. "Now go look at yourself in the pond," he said.

Lanny did, and he was surprised at what he saw. His wool was white like bleach. There was no trace of the black. But his skin itched and burned for several days.

Soon, he forgot that he was a black sheep and took his place with his flock, but the sheering time came again, and his wool was again sheered from his body.

When they took off his wool, his skin was exposed. It was course and chapped. It cracked and bristled. His skin was so sensitive that even the air made it hurt.

As the hair grew back, it was like having thousands of little needles sticking into his skin.

The pain was so terrible that he went off by himself to cry.

Soon, the skin had begun healing, and he could move without wincing.

Just as he was starting to feel better, he was contacted by Jefferson and told that it was time to dye his wool again.

Lanny couldn't stand the thought of going through this again.

"I can't!" he bleated. "I just can't."

"But you must!" Jefferson said. "If you are to be a member of good standing with the flock and if you are to be acceptable to the good shepherd, then you must."

Lanny consented. It hurt. It was torture, and I again felt Lanny's agony in my dream. But he could not stand the thought of being an outcast for just one minute and believed the pain would be a small price to pay for acceptance.

Once again, sheering time came to the flock.

This time, Lanny could not take it another round of bleaching. He hurt more this time than he did last time.

As he spoke with the other sheep in his dislocated flock, they admitted that it got more challenging to do rather than easier. "The dye was hard on the skin," they told him, "but in the end, he would see that it was worth it." Lanny wondered if they believed that.

When approached again about the dye, Lanny refused.

"What?" his friends asked. "What do you mean you're not going to do it again? You're not going to risk being an outcast, are you? You're not going to risk the anger of the good shepherd, are you?"

But Lanny couldn't bear the thought of more bleach on his skin. It was just too painful.

He took a trip to visit the wise Ram.

The Ram listened to him carefully and then looked at him with great compassion. "I understand what you're going through," he said. "I have seen this before."

"You have?" Lanny asked.

"For some reason, nature mixes things up just a bit. I think it's because she likes variety. But instead of appreciating the added color, her creatures conclude that it results from some perversion or some error." Then he looked down at Lanny. "Come," he said. "Follow me."

Lanny followed him, and they walked through the meadow into another pasture.

In this pasture, Lanny noticed many black and white sheep, all living and playing together. Nobody seemed to care that they were different. If anything, they enjoyed the differences and made light of them.

When Lanny was introduced, the rest of the flock welcomed him. "Welcome," they all said. "Come join us down at the pond."

Lanny remembered the pond. He had grown to hate the pond because it continued to show him how different he was from his friends and family. But this time, the pond made no judgments. He had black wool, and nobody else seemed to mind.

Lanny was home, and in my dream, I was happy that things finally worked out for him.

Meanwhile, the sheep in Lanny's former flock, including his mother and father and brothers and sisters, went on with their business, never knowing the pain they had caused, and they soon forgot all about Lanny.

I woke up smiling that morning because I knew Lanny would be okay with his new family: a family that loved him, black wool and all.